10 LEADING TOOLS

Rules, Tools & Habits
for Leading Yourself and Leading Others

The author has made every effort to acknowledge copyright holders for the material used or referenced in this book. Any person or organization that may have been overlooked should contact the author at:
info@kgbutlermedia.com

*10 Leading Tools: Rules, Tools & Habits for
Leading Yourself and Leading Others*

Copyright © 2022 KG Butler

All rights reserved. No part of this book may be reproduced in any form or by any means—whether electronic, digital, mechanical, or otherwise—without permission in writing from the publisher, except by a reviewer, who may quote
brief passages in a review.
All inquiries should be made to the author at:
info@kgbutlermedia.com

Library of Congress Control Number:

ISBN: 978-0-6454611-0-7
eBook ISBN: 978-0-6454611-1-4

Cover design by Hina Shakti

Printed in the United States of America

All events mentioned in this book are true to the best of the author's memory. It reflects the author's current recollection of the events and experiences over time. However, some timelines and dialog have been condensed for the purposes of the book. Many names and identifying characteristics have been changed to
avoid hurting anyone.

10 LEADING TOOLS

RULES, TOOLS & HABITS
FOR LEADING YOURSELF AND
LEADING OTHERS

KG BUTLER

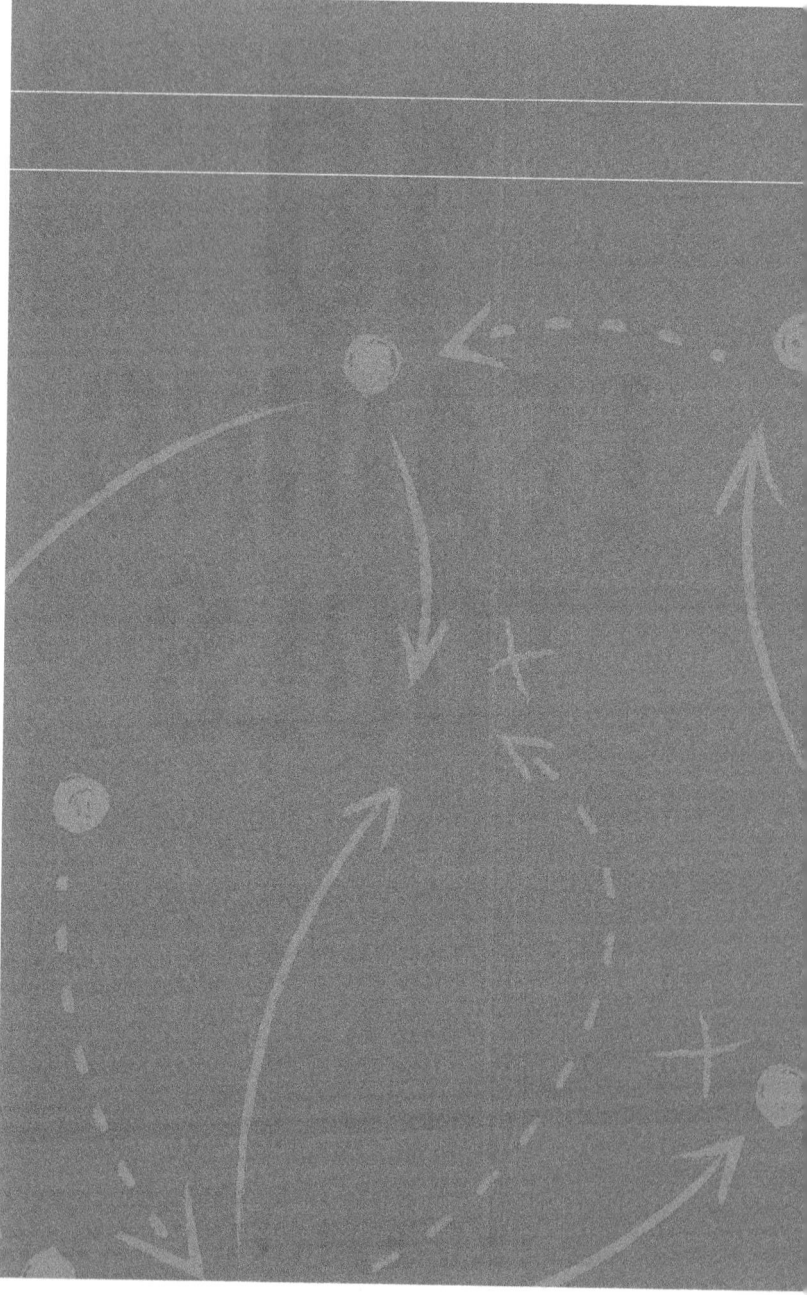

CONTENTS

INTRODUCTION
The Importance of Tools — 7

THE JOURNEY
Oh no, what is he doing? — 13

PART 1: ABOUT LEADERSHIP
What does it mean to be a leader every day? — 27

PART 2: THE TOOLS

TOOL #1	Use Purpose Over Task	43
TOOL #2	Learn a New Language	61
TOOL #3	Tell Different Stories	81
TOOL #4	Create Currents	99
TOOL #5	Play (PLAy)	117
TOOL #6	Pulse	133
TOOL #7	Be Vanilla	149
TOOL #8	Be Agile	165
TOOL #9	Be Real	183
TOOL #10	Be Bold	197

CONCLUSION
Think Differently — 211

Notes — 221
Index — 233

> **IF YOU GIVE THEM TOOLS, THEY'LL DO WONDERFUL THINGS WITH THEM.**

INTRODUCTION

The Importance of Tools

In 1994, *Rolling Stone* magazine columnist Jeff Goodell sat down to interview the CEO of NeXT Inc., an American technology company that developed the NeXT Computer. This was during the era when the personal computer and technology revolutions were in full swing, and the Internet was still in its fledgling stages. The thirty-nine-year-old CEO of the technology start-up was being interviewed as one of the leading technology visionaries of his time. He'd witnessed the heights of success from rival organizations like Microsoft, Apple, and IBM. Still, he vowed to carve a niche for his company by creating the next generation of personal computers that were so powerful, beautiful, and insanely great that they would put all other PCs to shame. Although the CEO's ambition was bold, it was almost expected from someone who was once touted as the entrepreneur of the decade just five years earlier. While doing research for this book, what caught my attention was the CEO's response to the question, "Do you still have as much faith in technology today as you did when you started out twenty years ago?" "Technology is nothing," he answered. "What's important is that you have a faith in people, that they're basically good and smart, and if you give them tools, they'll do wonderful things with them."

I could not agree more. This belief in what people can accomplish when given the right tools is not only profound; it's one of the central themes of this book. By the way, that CEO's name was Steve Jobs. Although his vision for NeXT Computer was never realized, Jobs used his forward-thinking to lead a new technology revolution for more than a decade after taking the helm at Apple with the introduction of the iPhone, iPad, and other innovations before his death of pancreatic cancer at age fifty-six.

Do you ever wonder why some people have the guts to challenge the status quo by doing something radically different while others don't? Or how some leaders inspire and create a mass of loyal followers while other leaders fail to motivate? Ever wonder how to make better or faster decisions for your team or family? Or how to better connect and communicate with your peers? *10 Leading Tools* will provide you with the keys to answer these questions and support the challenges of growing leaders. This book will also demonstrate effective leadership skills, reveal inventive ways of thinking, and offer the tools to help you do "wonderful things" by leading yourself and leading others around you.

WHAT'S A TOOL?

You will find many standard definitions of a *tool* when you do an online search, but before you get too attached to those definitions, take a journey with me. Most explanations about tools will describe a device, an instrument, or an implement used to carry out a particular function or task. If I were to ask you to think of some tools, what would you imagine? Most people will picture a hammer, a screwdriver, a wrench, a shovel, or other domestic devices. Some imaginative folks may have envisioned different utilitarian tools, such as a computer, mobile phone, or a pencil. These are all reasonable examples of tools, but I have a slightly different view. The following is my simplified definition for the purposes of this book: "A tool is anything used for our benefit."

This definition is more useful because tools can be almost anything, not just something with a physical form, like a hammer or a wrench. When Steve Jobs said, "Give them tools, and they'll do wonderful things with them," he was likely extolling more than physical tools to help people succeed. Yes, a tool can also be an idea, a shared vision, or a set of principles that help us accomplish things or complete a task. Think about it. We use tools like songs and rhymes to help our children better recall the alphabet. We use phrases like "righty tighty" or "lefty loosey" as tools to help us remember which direction to twist when opening a jar of pickles. Pioneers like Rosa Parks used an idea like the Montgomery bus boycott as a tool to galvanize a movement.

We have tools all around us, but there are many instances when we would not necessarily recognize something as a tool. Don't believe me? Step back in time and think about our early

Stone Age ancestors. Now try to imagine 2.6 million years ago, which is about the time when early stone toolmaking began, according to the Smithsonian. Do you know when the stone became sharpened and shaped to become the tip of an arrow? Or when people started to use rocks as blunt instruments for hammering? Stone did not miraculously appear in the shape of an arrowhead or drop from the sky already formed like a hammer. Boulders, rocks, stones, and pebbles have been part of the Earth's substance for billions of years. They have existed as part of the landscape of man since the beginning of time. Whether you believe in Adam and Eve or Darwin's theory of evolution, those solid, mineral-rich objects have always been around. No, the stone did not change. As humans, our perspective of what the stone could be or what it could do for us shifted. At some point, we began to see the stone as something new. As a species, in order to evolve, something or someone sparked the imaginations of our ancestors so they could envision the lowly stone as a tool that could benefit their lives and support their survival. We realized that it could be used as a tool, as an implement, and eventually as a weapon like the sharpened stone of an arrowhead or the five smooth stones launched by David to slay Goliath. This is the power of tools in the hands of humans. This is the power of tools in the hands of a leader.

It's important to understand, though, that *10 Leading Tools* is not simply about the tools; it's about people. It's about you. It's about helping you imagine and discover the utility of the tools already at your disposal. It's about helping you develop the skills to use those tools in the context of your career, family, and community. As you read the pages of the book, my goal is to help you see things differently by opening your eyes to how to effectively use the tools around you. When you can imagine yourself and the world differently, it frees you to take action and make those tools infinitely more helpful. This book will expose you to some of the most effective and well-researched tools of great leaders, tools that will enable you to grow your skills to be the leader, the parent, or the colleague you've always dreamed of becoming.

There is no doubt the tools in this book can be both powerful and transformative. But first, we must embrace the potential for change in our world. In the chapters to follow, we will explore ways to change how you think about leadership and what a leader should be. We'll discover how to take some presumably ordinary things and turn them into life-altering tools of leadership. We'll also learn critical skills for thriving in the face of change. Former President John F. Kennedy said, "Change is the law of life. And those who look only to the past or present are certain to miss the future." Let's look to the future together.

> THE SUCCESS QUEST
>
> IS INDEED A JOURNEY.

THE JOURNEY

Oh no! What is he doing?

After more than twenty-five years of working for businesses and consulting for companies of all sizes (from multibillion-dollar banks to mom-and-pop retailers to software start-ups and everything in between), in many ways, I have learned so little. No, I'm not afraid to admit that I'm still in the start-up phase of my learning journey, especially in the areas of leading. During my time as a business leader, I can proudly say that I have achieved a reasonable level of success, helping to lead and transform dozens of teams and organizations to work smarter and faster. I've also had the privilege of consulting for dozens of iconic brands like Oracle, Polaroid, Air New Zealand, and Apple. But it feels like baby steps compared to the size of the prize. I still feel like a toddler, stumbling my way through this leadership journey. Of course, success is always relative, but for me, hailing from a small town in Texas, making the leap to settle in Australia is a semblance of achievement. Success is a matter of perspective, and any sense of realized success is fleeting, so the success quest is indeed a journey.

My journey, like yours, has been a long, winding road full of surprises that now fills me with the light and shade of experience. The path I've traveled has taken me to Sydney, Australia, where I currently live with my wife and son. But before marriage, before my role as a husband and father, before starting a TV production company, before my appointment as general manager of a global consulting firm, I've long sought and wished to be a better leader. In my quest to know more, I studied thousands of years of leadership history. I've researched the rich and varied stories of famous leaders, from the likes of Marcus Atilius Regulus, a Roman general who served as consul in 256 BC, to Mother Theresa, to Martin Luther King Jr.

Along with my leadership pursuits in academia, I've personally led and been led by both effective and ineffective leaders. I've had the honor of leading teams of hundreds to help transform organizations and create award-winning products with many multinational companies. I've published articles about great leaders and taught tens of thousands of students in my leadership courses and workshops. I've worked for companies that have provided pathways to work beside, or be led by, some fantastic leaders. But this book is not about what I've learned from one company, one leader, one book, or one university study. This book is a culmination of all those things and more. In these pages, I ponder over the questions that still plague me as well as the lessons I've learned. It is a collection of years of taking small notes, asking tough questions, making mistakes, learning lessons, and integrating the countless nuggets of wisdom I've gleaned from those around me.

However, I can't say that I've always been interested in leaders, leading, or leadership. But I know that deep within my soul, I was always searching for "something." I gained the clarity of that *something* on a road trip to Augusta, Georgia, in mid-2000. And I've been forever changed because of it.

THE ROAD TO AUGUSTA: BYSTANDER NO MORE

I'm not a golfer, but even I recognize Augusta, Georgia, as the home of The Masters, the legendary golf tournament, that has become part of golfing folklore since the 1930s. My leadership journey began with a boy's trip from the Dallas area to Augusta in the summer of 2000 to visit my older brother. I'm the youngest of four children, three of whom are boys: Mark is the oldest, and Rick is in the middle. I always idolized Mark, who rose to be a local high school football legend in the town where we grew up. Mark had moved to Augusta for work, so Rick and I decided to take a trip to visit our big brother. Rick is a witty, sharp-tongued, charismatic type, who has a clever way with words. Growing up with these two was always mildly intimidating since I wasn't a football star nor as funny and charming as my other brother. I was not devoid of my own talents, but I would say my skills were less visible. My incognito superpower was that I was always a good student. Yes, that's it. I was the academic one. But in reality, that wasn't even my claim to family fame either. My older sister, Cheryl, is actually the academic among us. She went on to become the only college graduate in the family and now works as a paralegal.

Getting back to the road trip . . . Boy, it was a long drive, but Rick and I were prepared for it. It was a fourteen-hour journey from Rockwall, Texas, east of Dallas, to the city of Augusta, but we were well organized. We had made this journey before as a family when Mark first moved to Augusta, but this was the first time we tackled the journey as two young adults. We knew the trip was physically tiring, but it was generally a straightforward one.

On a cloudless Friday morning, we drove via US Interstate 20 and continued traveling east through Louisiana, Mississippi, Alabama, and eventually made our way into the Empire State of the South: Georgia. Rick started driving our Thrifty rental car as we departed at the crack of dawn from our mom's house, which is thirty minutes outside of Dallas. We both had our own vehicles, but we were not confident that either of our older model cars could survive the long trip. We switched drivers and stopped to eat lunch, refuel, and relax for the all-important bio-break after reaching the halfway point of Jackson, Mississippi. After our short pit stop, I was at the wheel and responsible for the trip's final leg, while Rick was tasked with DJ duty and navigation. I drove for several hours, and the passing highway sign showed that we were less than 150 miles from Augusta. With less than two hours remaining, that feeling of road trip optimism started to come over us. We were happy that our long journey was almost complete and felt all of the planning and preparation was worth it. It was during this last leg of our trip when it happened. As we traveled diligently along the highway through DeKalb County, Georgia, everything changed.

Our journey continued while listening to Rick's latest mix of R&B tunes that included tracks like "No More" by Ruff Endz,

"Country Grammar" by Nelly, and the "Thong Song" by Sisqó. We were delirious with fatigue and excitement when Rick noticed something ahead.

"Oh my God. What is he doing?" Rick exclaimed.

Ahead of us on the highway, we could see a midsized Dodge truck weaving quite erratically a few car lengths ahead. The driver moved left and right between lanes, forcing drivers around the truck to avoid a collision. As we motored down the highway at just above seventy miles per hour, there was now a chorus of horns and screeching tires as we all tried to evade what was occurring up ahead.

As we continued forward, the weaving truck was now only a short distance ahead of us. We could see the driver was a man, partially slumped forward in the driver's seat. It was evident that something was wrong. To this day, I can't tell you why he was driving so erratically. Was he intoxicated? Was he having a medical crisis? We'll never know, but the weaving continued, and now the truck was too close to us. The erratic driving was now close enough to hit us, so I had to do something.

"I've gotta get past him," I announced to Rick as my boot pressed deep into the accelerator of our rented Ford Taurus. I passed to the right of the truck just as he swerved to the left. It was scary, but I successfully maneuvered it.

We were then about two car lengths ahead of the erratic truck on the road, which seemed like the safest place to be. As I tried to focus on the road ahead, it happened. The truck weaved to the right, then overcorrected to the left.

"Oh no! What is he doing? No! Oh no!" Rick exclaimed as he looked back at the truck. *Crash*.

The truck struck the outside concrete barrier of the motorway, then bounced back violently across four lanes of traffic and started a death roll. It flipped in the air and rolled over and over and over. I slammed on the brakes as I watched it all unfold from the rearview mirror. It was hard to believe what we had just witnessed. We barely escaped being hit by the driver. We also couldn't fathom how no other vehicles were involved in the accident while the truck pinballed across I-20. What we witnessed was no mere car crash. It was a demolition. Once the mangled Dodge came to a rest near the median, I immediately pulled over to the side of the highway.

Still in shock from what we had just witnessed, I said a silent prayer, "God, let him be okay. Please help him."

After the paramedics arrived and we provided the Georgia highway patrol with our version of events, we made our way to Augusta. As we traveled east the last two hours, Rick and I didn't speak much. We didn't say anything about the crash. I guess we were both processing the tragedy we had just witnessed.

Later that evening, we made it to Augusta, The Master's city. We only briefly mentioned the accident to Mark and how it had delayed our arrival, then unpacked and settled into the house for our brotherhood weekend. Mark treated us to an unforgettable meal and looked after us like only a big brother could. But as the sun receded on the day and I lay alone under the dark of night, my mind began to wonder. What just happened? Why were we there at the exact moment of the accident? What was I meant to learn from the accident? How lucky are we to have survived? Could I have done more to help? Spontaneously, tears filled my vision. As much as I tried,

I could not stop the well of tears from running down my face. It felt as if the stream of hot, wet tears had been dammed off for a lifetime. I cried tears for the years of doubt, tears for the years of denial. I wept for all of the things I had been and for what I was yet to become. I cried myself to sleep. From that moment, my vision became clear. I knew I could no longer be a bystander.

The dramatic end to this story can be found in Tool# 10. But for those of you who can resist the urge to skip ahead, I'll explain how this incident sparked a flame in my journey as a leader, as well as how to get the most benefit from this book.

MY JOURNEY

The next day, I awoke on my brother's sofa feeling fresh and grateful for the day. As I recalled the past day, it prompted me to rethink my role and goals in life. My main questions were: "Am I doing enough in this world? Am I fully contributing?"

At this point in my life, I had graduated high school, completed a couple of years at university, and landed an excellent job as a technology consultant. My original grand plan was to finish my degree by continuing college part-time while working the job of my dreams, but that never happened. I became a so-called road warrior, the self-proclaimed title assigned to us consultants who spent more than 50 percent of our time on the road—or, in my case, on flights and in hotels. I was traveling 90 percent of the time, but I didn't mind. I was living the life. I was a young, naive consultant flying to a new client site each week. My technology specialization was in high demand, so I took full advantage of the opportunity. As a consultant for a software company, I would leave my home near Dallas-Fort Worth International Airport on a Monday morning and spend the week working with clients large and small. My life of traveling around the country seemed unreal to this small-town boy, as I visited dozens of cities in far-flung corners of the country like Chicago, Illinois; Dearborn, Michigan; and Ocean City, Maryland. In my head, I had "made it." I felt like I was living my best life until that moment on the path to Augusta.

It was during this time in my life that I began to seek more. In the beginning, it was all about career goals. Within weeks, I had applied for and landed a management role with the consulting firm, but that wasn't enough. Then I wanted to find love and settle into a community. I stopped traveling and soon met the love of my life: my wife, Jillian, an Australian with a passion for food, travel, and adventure. Maybe the accident made me think of my mortality, or perhaps I was suffering from some version of post-traumatic stress, or maybe I was now simply awake. Whatever the reason, I now vowed to learn more, do more, and experience more. I was determined to learn more about myself, about people, and this is how I stumbled into the world of leaders and leadership. Yes, my leadership journey began by simply wanting to learn and form better connections with the people around me. At first, I sought to connect with those men and women I felt could mentor and guide me. It was through those initial bonds that I started to value relationships of all kinds. For a whole series of reasons that likely requires years of professional therapy to understand, I yearned to connect and create lasting relationships.

Through exercising these close relationships and connections, I began to see myself as a good leader of others. I was not a good leader because I was suddenly winning leadership awards or getting promoted to a senior role in a prestigious organization. I was a good leader because I now felt comfortable in my own skin. I was now comfortable speaking up, standing firm, or just listening. I was ready to both actively lead and be shepherded by others. I would no longer settle for being a witness to life or reporting from the sidelines. I wanted to be an active participant. That is why this book exists. My heartfelt hope is that the tools in this book will, in some small way, help fan the flame or ignite the fire of other leaders, especially the reluctant ones.

HOW TO USE THIS BOOK

Maybe the best way to start is by telling you how not to use this book. Do not use this book as any type of step-by-step guide to management. 10 Leading Tools will not tell you how to do your status reporting at the office, how to deliver better presentations, or how to give feedback to staff. However, this book should be used as a reference point for research that supports key leadership principles, or as a source of coaching and encouragement in your leadership journey. The book can and should be used to remind you of where you'd like to be as a leader. 10 Leading Tools, which I'll refer to as "10LT," is not only for experienced leaders or even leaders-in-training. It's for anyone who wants to improve their life through self-reflection and action. 10LT is for anyone looking to expand their thinking and grow as a person.

Another thing to note about using this book is that 10LT consists of two main parts. The first part is an introduction to helpful leadership styles and some new leadership concepts (About Leadership). The second part of the book begins with the list of tools, starting with Tool# 1. To make this book more useful to leaders of all levels, I'm going to suggest something that may seem unconventional as the author. I suggest that some of you skip ahead to "Part 2", the list of tools, if leadership theory is not "your thing," or if you are already quite familiar with modern concepts of leadership in your family, career, and community. My suggestion to skip ahead is not because I don't think those aspects of the book are helpful—because I do. Frankly, I believe they are some of the most insightful parts of the book and will provide useful background and context for any leader. However, I also understand the harsh realities of having a time-poor life. So, in an attempt to give some of you the opportunity to get straight into the book's namesake, feel free to fast-forward to the tools—guilt-free. You have my blessing.

I have another tip for those who may not have the time or inclination to read the entire book, immediately. Although the tools have a natural progression, the order is less relevant. Each tool within 10LT ends with a retrospective section, which is a summary of the key themes and some practical suggestions on applying that tool in your everyday life. Since each tool largely stands alone, thumbing through these key themes may help those time-challenged people trying to decide which tools are the most relevant or helpful for their current journey as a leader. Think of it like reading the episode descriptions of your favorite podcast and downloading the most interesting ones before subscribing to the channel. As an author, I want you to lovingly read every word of this book, but as a leader, I'd rather empower you to make the choices that make the most sense for you.

IT'S AN INSIDE JOB

Lastly, before we dive into the next part of this journey together, I want to mention one more fundamental aspect to make these tools more effective. As you read about these rules, tools, and habits, I don't want you to judge them based on who you are now. I want you to look at them in light of who you want to be. It can take time to develop all of these skills, so don't fret if something doesn't resonate or work for you immediately. Persevere, and the rewards will be worth it.

As you discover the tools in this book, there doesn't have to be an immediate outward reflection of change, growth, or revelation. There merely needs to be a slight shift in your thinking, opening your mind to what you want to be or what could be. Understanding the concept of an incremental shift is how you will get the most benefit from this book.

That means you must have a good relationship with yourself. You must be able to look at yourself in the mirror and decide where you want to be. I know this is an uncomfortable position to be in. It's also particularly awkward to stand in front of one's own mirror and ask, "What and who do I want to be?" But this is the type of conversation you need to have with yourself in order to grow. Go ahead, do it now. I'll wait . . . That wasn't so bad, was it?

Now, remember your goal (your answer to the question) as

you start working your way through the 10LTs. Whatever you want to become, the result will be personal growth and expansion, which ripples into leading yourself and your tribe more effectively. You will then be equipped to positively influence and impact your career, family, and community. That is the ideal result. That's the challenge. That's the next goal in your journey. So let's get started!

PART 1

ABOUT LEADERSHIP

> LEADERS ARE WHO WE ARE, NOT THE RESULT OF WHAT WE DO.

What does it mean to be a leader every day?

We'll dive into the tools of *10 Leading Tools* shortly. But before we do, it's worth understanding more about the notion of leadership, leading, and leaders. My interest in learning about leadership came relatively late in life, and maybe that's why it was so difficult to reconcile. Maybe it was a case of trying to teach this old dog new tricks. At every turn in my learning, I uncovered more questions than answers. American scholar and author Warren G. Bennis described it best when he wrote, "Of all the hazy and confounding areas in social psychology, leadership theory undoubtedly contends for top nomination. And, ironically, probably more has been written and less is known about leadership than about any other topic in the behavioral sciences." But through the confusion and ambiguity, I persevered. The need to understand more about myself and the simple desire to be the best consultant, coworker, or manager for the people I worked with continued to fuel my hunger.

LEADERSHIP THEORIES

With a thirst for knowledge, I studied models like the Great Man Theory. This theory emerged in the nineteenth century and suggested that a person's natural abilities and attributes, man or woman, propel them to their rightful position to reign over others. It describes great leaders as being born with superior intellect, heroism, charisma, or inspirational abilities. This one was a bit disheartening because if one had to be born with these traits, I was surely in trouble.

I looked at the leadership studies of psychologist Kurt Lewin. Lewin had a different view on leadership in the 1930s when he outlined the most widely accepted leadership styles. Lewin's influence introduced us to three of the most common styles: autocratic, democratic, and laissez-faire. Without going into academic overload, I'll explain the core themes of each style.

An autocratic leader, also known as an authoritarian leader, is the type of leader who likes to control a situation. We have all known leaders or bosses like this, or maybe even someone in our family. You are probably more familiar with that person being called terms like bossy, micromanager, or a know-it-all. If you've ever described someone by saying, "She has to have it her way," that's an autocratic characteristic. In truth, if we are honest with ourselves, we may all possess a little autocratic-ness when it comes to the things we are most passionate about. Although the autocratic style generally gets a bad rap, these leaders are quite effective when quick decisions are required in a given situation.

Lewin also detailed the democratic leadership style, which prefers to have the group or team involved in decision-making.

This democratic style is also known as a participative leadership style since team participation and collaboration are at the center of this approach. The democratic leader is often popular amongst teams, but decision-making is often a challenge when trying to consider various opinions. Lewin also introduced the concept of the laissez-faire leader, or as I like to call it, the laid-back leader. Laissez-faire is a French term that loosely translates to "let it be" or "leave it alone," so the leader's mode of operation is often noticeably hands-off. This approach can be good for an already high-performing team or experts, but in other settings, a lack of accountability, coaching, and guidance may cause a team to struggle to achieve certain goals.

Lewin's styles became quite helpful to the business world as they made specific behaviors in leaders easy to identify. These styles made way for a slew of more contemporary and nuanced versions like situational, supportive, transactional, pacesetter, and servant leadership styles. Like many growing leaders, having insights into the various styles was a great way to start seeing leadership around me. I would recommend the same for anyone just starting their leadership journey. Aligning a leadership style to a behavior recognized in yourself, a neighbor, or coworkers will go a long way toward making the concepts real and more attainable. Through learning more about the different leadership styles, I identified myself as part supportive and part democratic. Still, I had many shades of others, such as servant, laissez-faire, and autocratic. Do you see yourself in any of these leadership styles?

If you want to know more about leadership styles in general or learn more about your own style, search for "leaders toolbelt leadership styles." There you'll find my blog, which has detailed articles and examples of each leadership style, along with a quiz on how to determine your predominant style.

Reading literature, academic studies, and countless articles allowed me to look at the world around me from a different perspective. I started to look at leadership as less about heroism, lofty titles, and something only a few "great men" could achieve and instead focused on the everyday aspects of being a leader. In essence, I discovered that leadership was not what I thought it was. I found there were many leadership beliefs, idioms, and ideas to learn and unlearn.

DEBUGGING THE CODE

My professional consulting career began in a specialized area of technology called software testing and quality assurance. For those not familiar with information technology, my job (and my team's job) was to find all of the defects, bugs, and issues in a product before an end-user or customer encountered them. For example, if a company was launching a new clothing website in a month, my teams would spend hours, days, and weeks testing all of the features. Before the general public could start using the site, testers navigated the online shopping cart, clicked all the buttons and links, checked the spelling, and reported any issues that the site programmers and developers needed to resolve. The best software testers were always the inquisitive ones who did the things that customers shouldn't do, so we benefited from them thinking outside the box. These software testers were the most valuable because they helped companies resolve the most obscure issues before real customers had to experience them. As my interest in the history of leaders and leadership grew, I started using my background as a tester to think about leadership differently. I wanted to debug or deconstruct the product I was "being sold" to understand how it really worked.

During this time, I noticed a peculiar pattern in how leadership models have been developed. When I looked at the evolution of these models, the research, and the conversation, the obvious pattern was that, historically, they were created by "old white men" (although there's nothing wrong with that). But a secondary pattern emerged as well. No matter how eloquently the model was articulated or how insightful the position, the context typically described leadership in terms of what I would define as one's profession, job, or career—examples of such being presidents, CEOs, generals in battle, heads of state, and so on. But as I dove into the research and combined it with my personal experiences, I discovered another pattern as I began to compare leaders against my own life and life in the twenty-first century. I found that leadership happens all around us—in our neighborhoods, in our multicultural communities, and within businesses.

I watched as great leaders emerged in my life; past and present, they were all around me. Leaders were not always on television, on the battlefield, or on the sports field. Leading was happening in my family. Leading was happening in my local church and in my community soccer league. Yes, leadership was happening in business meetings and boardrooms as well. But that wasn't the only place, as I had previously been led to believe. I began to recognize all of the leadership behaviors and styles in people that lived average lives. As I took notes, as I watched in silence, as I considered all that I had observed over the years, I realized that being a leader is not one-dimensional. Leaders perform the act of leadership in many different ways as they tap into the different facets of their lives. I realized that being a leader has a situational aspect. Leadership has context.

What is context? The *Cambridge Dictionary* describes context as "the situation within which something exists or happens, and that can help explain it." I can imagine that some of you are saying, "Thanks, KG. That's cool, but I could have Googled that myself. But what does that really mean? Especially in relation to this leadership stuff?" It simply means that leadership occurs in different situations, and leaders are not the same types of leaders in all situations. It means that a leader who is an autocratic leader at the office may be a democratic leader or a laissez-faire leader at home. It means that leadership can occur in the local bridge club as well as the city council meeting. It means that as a leader, understanding your circumstances and changing with them is as important as understanding your core leadership style or default behavior.

This concept of adapting your leadership style was first popularized by Paul Hersey and Ken Blanchard when they introduced the Situational Leadership Theory in the 1960s and '70s. Their theory was first introduced as part of the book *Management of Organizational Behavior*. Although it has changed and morphed over the years, it is designed to better understand workplace leadership. The Situational Leadership Model provides a framework between leaders and followers that guides them through an intricate grid of various quadrants of influence behaviors. It suggests that leaders change and flex between four specific behaviors: Delegating, Participating, Selling, and Telling.

The model introduced by Hersey and Blanchard was thorough and insightful, but I felt like it was still missing something. I loved the thought of leadership adapting to the current situation. That just seemed right. No one has the same behavior or style in all situations. People just aren't wired that way. I liked the concept, but as I tried to apply it to my life and others in my life, I always wanted more. Again, like many theories and models, it seemed to be inadvertently complex and steered toward theoretic workplace practices and styles of behavior. As I tried to teach these concepts to others, I realized they needed to be more accessible. Whether in mentoring and training or in the process of learning, I longed for a leadership method that simplified things. I needed a model in which the concepts were both practical and applicable to all leaders, young and old.

Maybe it was the software tester's curiosity in me, or perhaps it was sheer audacity, but I couldn't let it rest. There was a piece of the puzzle missing beyond the various leadership styles. I continued to search and experiment with concepts. As I grew in understanding, I started to recognize a few overriding contextual influences that had the most impact on which leadership style we applied to a given situation. Over the years, my research has pointed to the realization that the context of everyday leadership typically falls into one of three areas: leading in our career, leading in our family, or leading in our community. When I understood the relationship between the three contextual areas of leadership, I knew I had found my missing link. Our leadership styles are actively engaged within the context of our career, family, or community, which I call the leader's triangle.

Every day, we have the opportunity to lead in one of these areas. This concept changed everything for me. The revelation was profound. I could now fully connect the dots between the leadership styles and the associated context as part of an overarching concept I call the Modern Leaders Model. This model has helped me teach others that we invoke various leadership styles at many levels within our lives, not exclusively within our careers.

MODERN LEADERS MODEL

For those who study and follow the academic aspects of leadership, the concepts included in this model should seem incredibly familiar. Yes, the pieces of the puzzle have always been on the table. By introducing the Modern Leaders Model, I'm simply trying to connect the straight-edged puzzle pieces with its corners to create a new frame. This model is in no way meant to replace or displace any of the existing theories. As I stated before, there has been a phenomenal amount of research, a plethora of publications, and countless books on leading, leaders, and leadership. This model is designed to add a new dimension to a discipline that has always been understood but rarely articulated. While most studies try to answer, "What is leadership?" I set out to answer a different question: "What does it mean to be a leader every day?" The Modern Leaders Model is about helping leaders find that answer. It's about helping people. That's it. It is not about an unhealthy obsession with theories, academia, or theology. The model is a realistic view of what it means to be a leader in today's world. I named it the Modern Leaders Model in an attempt to bring our thoughts, our vision, and our view of leaders forward. I know it is not perfect, but I pray it is a shift in the right direction.

Those readers who are students of leadership will notice the use of the word "leaders" instead of "leadership" in the name of the model. This is a nuance I can explain. When I was growing up, the word leadership always had this unspoken barrier; it created a physiological separation between who I was and who I could be. Leadership has always felt like the mystical culmination of the things you do, the years you serve, and the title you've earned. It felt like leadership resulted from something that a worker, a soldier, a politician, a boss, or a manager may do or achieve. For example, saying, "She is now in a leadership position" implies a role. The term "leaders," on the other hand, define people instead of a role. Leaders are caring. They feel. Leaders are who we are, not the result of what we do. It's like me being Kerry G. Butler. That's just who I am, and I don't need to do anything specific to be me. Once acknowledged, being a leader is just like that. No one can take that away from you.

The Modern Leaders Model is made up of three layers—with your career, your family, and your community sitting at the top. The modern elements in the middle let you know in what ways you are leading: connection, communication, curiosity, commitment, and context. Finally, there are the various approaches, behaviors, and styles of leadership, like autocratic, charismatic, and democratic leadership. Although we will not cover the details of the full model in this book, there is value in understanding the relationship between career, family, and community to gain the most benefit from the tools that follow.

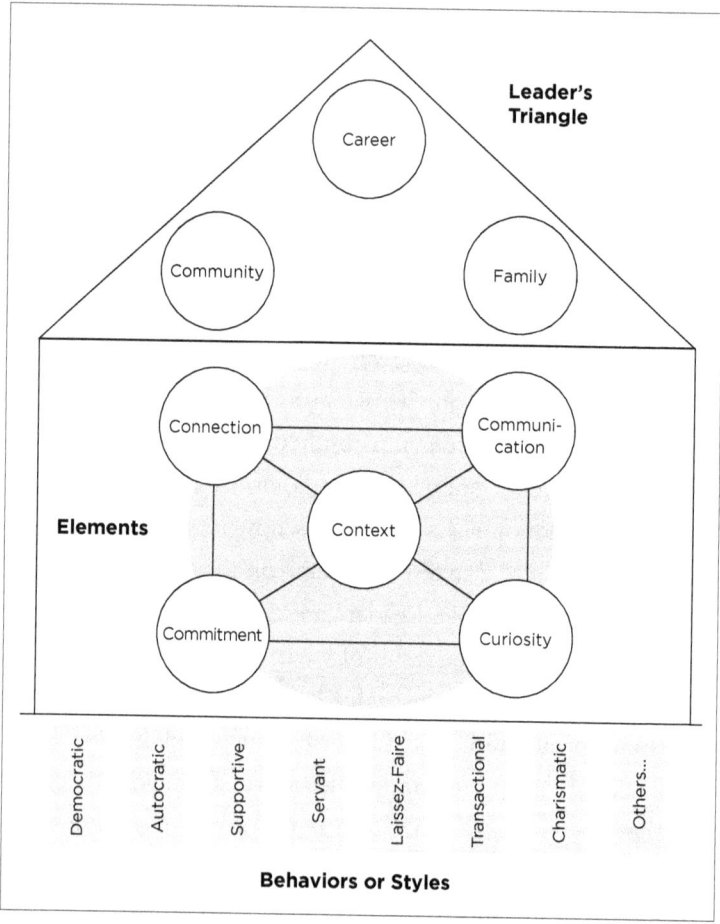

Fig. 1 Modern Leaders Model diagram.

LEADER'S TRIANGLE

The delineation between career, family, and community is not meant to be revolutionary. Instead, it's to help us evolve into the modern way we approach leadership. Aside from career, family, and community, there are many sub-areas where we exhibit leadership. Still, I find that most will fall into one of these three buckets that I call the Leader's Triangle.

Career

As I mentioned before, the path to career leadership is well-worn. There is plenty of great literature devoted to the subject, so I won't spend much time on the dimension of your career other than to say this: Your career can be an important aspect of your existence, but now it's time to provide equal airtime to other key aspects of your life. Think about the introduction to this book, or any other nonfiction book, for that matter. No matter how I resisted, I introduced you to who I am, KG Butler, by including elements of my career. For better or worse, our career is a big part of our identity. It cannot and should not be ignored when it comes to developing yourself as a leader. But for those of you who may have mistakenly put too much stock into your career, use this model to remind yourself of the other vital aspects of your leadership capability that you have likely overlooked—family and community.

Family

The notion of family is also stating the obvious when it comes to leadership. Being a leader as we connect with those closest to us or those we are genetically linked with is likely the original form of leadership. As humans evolved into advanced beings on Earth, we led our family units as a natural mechanism to survive and thrive. Then Homo sapiens evolved to form broad communities, where leaders emerged long before the concept of a career existed.

The term "family" is not solely reserved for parents, siblings, cousins, or partners. It can also be used to describe our closest friends at university or our best mates that we hang out with on the weekends. "Family" describes the people in our tribe—our peeps—the people that we care for. As a leading structure, this is the most natural, which explains why we see this leadership formation in almost every primate. We see it in pods of dolphins. We see it in the wild cats of Africa. We see it in chimpanzees. All of these creatures have packs or family units, and within those family units, leaders emerge. Sometimes leadership emerges in the form of provision by gathering food. Other times, leadership is demonstrated by caring for the young or weak and protecting the pride, pod, or family unit in the face of danger. This sense of family, this connection, has always given us reason to lead.

Community

Then there's the context of "community." The context of community is a broad category that shows the connection to our outer circle. The *Oxford Dictionary* describes a community as "a group of people living in the same place or having a particular characteristic in common or the condition of sharing or having certain attitudes and interests in common." Sometimes we lead as part of a local association, sports team, or knitting group. You may be an usher at the local church or volunteer at your child's school. Nowadays, we can also lead our online community, whether you're offering courses on a platform like Udemy, providing tutorials on YouTube, or influencing Instagram or Facebook followers. Leading in the community is about connecting through our common interests, which binds us to others.

By applying this context lens to our lives and understanding the multiple situations in which we naturally lead, we can begin to acknowledge our roles as everyday leaders. Of course, knowing the context of the common situations where or when we lead helps us learn more about ourselves. But it doesn't always indicate we are leading—or does it? No, we are not always leading in our career, family, or community, but it is important to recognize the context of leaders. It is only through acknowledging the big or small leadership tendencies in our lives that we can start to hone in and improve upon those skills. By understanding the different aspects of the Leader's Triangle, we can now think differently about what it means to lead. We can reevaluate how we already lead in our daily lives. Many will realize that leading is less foreign to them than previously thought.

WHY DOES IT MATTER?

I can hear some of you saying, "That's mildly interesting, KG. But why does it matter? How does understanding the Leader's Triangle help me? How can I apply it to help me become a better leader for my team?"

We'll talk about this in more detail later in the book, but in short, knowing these aspects of modern leadership changes the way we think about ourselves and therefore rewires our brains to be better leaders. Simply knowing that you are already leading in multiple aspects of your life can help you recognize and practice leadership skills in more areas of your everyday existence. The practice or repetition of leadership starts to strengthen the connections in our brains called "neural pathways." These pathways become stronger and easier to access as our leadership habits grow, making us more confident and capable leaders.

As you continue reading this book, you will notice that many of the tools I offer are not new. These instruments already exist around us, but we may not have recognized them as tools that we can use for our benefit—tools we can use to accelerate our learning. Tools we can use to increase our capacity to lead. Tools we can use to inspire others. That's what we'll discover next as we dive into the 10 Tools.

There is something else that you should know as you learn more about the tools in this book. Tools are only tools when intentionality is expressed. In other words, we must be purposeful in our use of something to classify it as a tool. Taking us back to the example of the stone used by our ancestors, if the stone exists and there is no intention to use it for our benefit, then it's just a rock, right? But if we can see it and imagine its usefulness in solving a problem, then that intentionality is expressed. A tool is born. Use this book and the Modern Leaders Model in the same way. Take the information and see it in a new way. Be intentional.

PART 2

THE TOOLS

>

EFFORTS AND COURAGE ARE NOT ENOUGH WITHOUT PURPOSE AND DIRECTION.

—JOHN F. KENNEDY

TOOL #1

Use Purpose Over Task

THE HAPPIEST PLACE ON EARTH

It was a crisp summer morning in 1981, and I had barely slept a wink the night before. It wasn't my birthday, and it also wasn't Christmas, but my excitement boiled over with equal anticipation. All I could do was think about boarding the bus that morning. The bus was leaving at 6:00 a.m., and I wanted to make sure that I was ready. This was going to be a big day for me. It was the first time I would leave the comfort and security of my hometown, and I couldn't wait to experience the world.

You see, I grew up in a very small town that had all of the basic things my family and I needed. Rockwall, Texas, had a nice Brookshire Brothers grocery store, a Sonic Drive-In, and a brand new Walmart shopping center. There was no reason to leave Rockwall unless you were an adult and needed to travel thirty miles west to Dallas for work. This Saturday morning was off the charts in terms of excitement levels since it was the first time I would be traveling outside of the Dallas area. And not only outside of Dallas, Texas, but we were also traveling all the way to Disneyland in Anaheim, California, which was every young boy's dream.

During this childhood cross-country adventure, I understood the magic of Disney and all that it had to offer. This bus trip was taking us to "The Happiest Place on Earth," as it was termed. And the opportunity opened my yearning eyes like never before. For me, as a little boy, it wasn't simply the destination. It was the representation of a whole new world. A world that previously only existed on fuzzy Technicolor television screens. Although I was already beyond the age of obsessing over Mickey Mouse or Goofy, when I stepped through the gates of the theme park, I was in awe of everything. In awe of the spectacle, of the joy, of the pure magic that I experienced. In fact, the live version of the Magic Kingdom was even more magical than my sheltered brain could have imagined. There seemed to be an unspoken language in the park. A language of connection, of engagement. A language of wonder. In an instant, I transformed from a barefooted boy from Texas to a crooked-smiled youth, brimming with hope and curiosity. Suddenly, my world expanded, and I saw a land of possibilities. This fleeting brush with magic opened my eyes and shifted my view of reality, of what was possible. Even as a young boy, I sensed that life as I knew it would never be the same. For me, it was indeed the happiest place on earth.

THE FORMULA FOR HAPPINESS

Fast-forward to living in Australia thirty-plus years later, and I was fortunate enough to be involved with Disney again through their leadership and strategy training sessions. It was being held by one of the major banks that I worked for at the time. At this juncture in my career, I had participated in dozens of leadership training sessions, so I had little hope that this one would be different. But this session, much to my surprise, was a game-changer for me. It was through this session that I first learned the power of "purpose" as part of Tool #1.

The leadership training was facilitated by the Disney Institute. If you haven't heard of the Disney Institute, you are not alone. This was the first time I had heard of this renowned institution as well. Of course, I knew the name Disney, but I had never come across their institute for cast-member training. The bank had flown a team from Florida's Disney Institute over nine thousand miles to Sydney for a week-long series of intense leadership coaching sessions for their top leaders. It was through these sessions that I first learned of Disney's formula for creating happiness.

Today, Disney is a media and entertainment powerhouse and one of the most recognized brands on the planet. But its roots were planted a century ago when Walt Disney and his brother, Roy, started the Disney Brothers Studio in the early 1920s. The pair's success in animated feature-length films led Walt Disney to dream of creating a theme park filled with wonder and inspired by Disney's animated characters.

Walt's dream, Disneyland, was opened in July of 1955 in Anaheim, California. The phenomenal popularity of the park eventually spawned Disney World in Orlando, Florida, and other Disney-themed parks around the world, including Japan, France, and China. But what was their formula for success? More importantly, what could I learn from the business strategy of Disney? Honestly, I was skeptical, thinking the training wouldn't reveal anything of genuine interest, but I was more than pleasantly surprised.

The first day of the training was entertaining and insightful, to my delight. A pair of engaging presenters led us through a series of activities, presentations, and group exercises. The male and female tag team that led us were full of energy and information. The duo held our attention by drip-feeding us with a delightful mix of stories detailing the corporate history, while others spoke of their personal experiences. The types of unique experiences shared with us revealed the good and the bad of a leader's journey. Their honesty about the reality of leadership alluded to the cycle of real-world scares and restoration that leads to revelation and, ultimately, transformation. Yes, they were speaking about the ups and downs of the Walt Disney Company, but it felt genuine. The stories felt more like family history than typical company bylines. We were enthralled by the lessons on day one and were eager for more.

On the second day of the multi-day session, the stories they told profoundly impacted my life's journey. It inspired Tool #1, Use Purpose Over Task. As the session began, the room filled with leaders and aspiring leaders who were ripe with anticipation for the day ahead. The trainers stepped it up a notch by peppering us with various Disney paraphernalia and trinkets to encourage participation or as a reward when questions were answered correctly. In this day's session, we learned about the many company values that made Disney tick. In particular, we learned about one of the philosophies championed by Walt Disney from the beginning. Walt Disney believed that the secret to success in the theme parks was to allow each staff member to take personal responsibility for producing that sought-after "Disney magic" for guests.

INTRODUCING THE CAST

To understand the values that make Disney tick, our trainers explained that Disney implements a few small but clever things. First, all employees are known as "cast members" instead of staff. Disney believes that this simple nuance in language helps remind everyone that they are a part of the Disney production of happiness—a part of the performance, a part of creating magic for its customers. Another little touch is that everyone in the company wears nametags. The nametag displays the team members' names and where they are from. My nametag might read "KG: Dallas, Texas." This allows others on the team, as well as the guests of Disney, to have instant access to something about the staff, encouraging an immediate connection with the cast.

Also, for many years, Disney famously had every new cast member start by working in one of the Disney theme parks. Whether the cast member was a senior executive in the Disney animation studios or an administrative assistant, their first weeks with the company were spent directly understanding, experiencing, and creating the magic for customers. These were a few of the ways that described how Disney ensures the alignment of all cast members with Disney's core values and purpose.

To help drive this idea home and demonstrate the Disney values in action, one of the trainers told us a story about a Disney cast member named Jenny:

"Jenny was a loyal cast member who had been with Disney for over ten years. She was a valuable part of the janitorial and maintenance team at the Disney World Park in Orlando, Florida. Jenny and her team were a proud bunch that helped us ensure the parks were always sparkling clean."

She then directed our attention to the screens at the front of the room. There, she projected a photo of Jenny. The picture showed Jenny in her neat, white maintenance uniform, but she wasn't doing typical janitorial activities. The image presented to the room showed Jenny leading a group of young, smiling girls in what appeared to be a parade through the Boardwalk. There were three girls dressed in matching little enchanted fairy outfits. Jenny, not to be outdone, was poised in front of this single-file parade of marchers. She was proudly leading the girls through the streets of Disney World. But not like a typical, respectable maintenance worker with years of stellar experience. With her janitor's broomstick raised high in the air like a baton, Jenny was assuming the drum major position in this mini-marching band. It was an unexpected sight to see. A few chuckles sheepishly dotted the room as we examined the photo, not knowing if seriousness or levity was appropriate.

After a moment of pause, allowing the room to fully understand what they were seeing, the trainer began to pace the floor, and she questioned the room, "What do you see in the photo? What does Jenny look like she's doing?" You could again hear murmuring amongst the participants in the room, but there were no discernible answers. Finally, a voice from the back bellowed, "Looks like she doesn't know how to hold a broom," which was met by a small chorus of laughter.

"Okay, fair enough," said the trainer. "Any more thoughts?"

"People are laughing and having fun," said one of the participants.

"Good, any more thoughts?" Again, whispers were piercing the silence.

This time a female voice chimed in, "They're pretending to march in some sort of parade."

"Hmm, okay..." responded the trainer.

It was what I heard next that changed my thinking. It completely shifted how I understood *purpose*. And, more surprisingly, how purpose relates to all other aspects of life.

FROM OOPS TO OPPORTUNITY

As the trainer made her way to the center of the dimly-lit room, she proclaimed, "Let me tell you what we at Disney see. We see someone living one of our core values. We see Jenny doing what every cast member at Disney strives to do every day. Jenny is living the value of *task versus purpose*."

You could see the looks of both bewilderment and intrigue in the room. I was personally a little confused about that statement. How does a staff member doing everything but their job equate to living the core values of Disney? She continued:

> "See those smiles? That's the magic." She paused and pointed at the happy girls in the photo. "Let me tell you the full story of what you're seeing. The three little girls you see in the photo entered the park earlier that morning with their parents, full of excitement and eagerness to see the iconic Cinderella's Castle. As they made their way through the park, the family stopped to buy

the girls some ice cream treats. Two of the girls quickly finished their holiday treats, but one of the girls was still enjoying her favorite coconut-flavored ice cream cone when the unthinkable happened . . . *Splat!* She dropped her ice cream. Luckily, the team at Disney was on the case. Cleanliness is one of the cornerstones of Disneyland theme parks. So as soon as the ice cream hit the pavement, Jenny looked up from sweeping her designated area and noticed what just happened to the little girl and her ice cream. She quickly swooped in with every intention to clean the sticky mess from the cobblestone streets. But then Jenny realized that this little girl was crying her eyes out. As her parents were consoling the girl, Jenny thought to herself, *These little girls walked through the gates to experience the wonder of Disney World. The last thing they needed was to be upset by the dropped ice cream.* So Jenny made the extraordinary decision to comfort the little girl by leading her and the others down the Boardwalk in a parade to replace the fallen cone. Now think about that. Jenny had a job to do, which is what we paid her to do—clean the park," the trainer said, hoping she'd hit the mark on making her point.

"On the other hand, Jenny realized what was most important: To seize the opportunity to make magic happen. To help this young girl realize her dream was more important than the task of cleaning the pavement. She made the right decision to continue aligning with the purpose of Disney, which is to make it the happiest place on earth. So, in this instance, Jenny chose *purpose versus task.*"

Wow, my mind is blown, I thought as I sat in stone-faced silence amongst my peers. I could not tell if they all had the same revelation, but this was truly a game-changer for me. This was a simple tool that anyone could use to help guide their daily decisions. Jenny used it to help make sure she was aligned with Disney's purpose and values, but we can all use this as a tool for any position we find ourselves in.

As I started using this concept in my life, at client sites, and within my teams over the years, the tool evolved into what it is today, Purpose Over Task, or POT as I like to call it. Admittedly, the acronym already faces instant PR problems since the word "pot" has a long history of being associated with youth and hippie rebellion in society. But using the words "Purpose Over Task" as a mantra is just the opposite. POT can quickly help distill one's thinking and narrow a myriad of thoughts into crystal-clear perspective. It helps people align their purpose to their actions with simplistic elegance.

Using Purpose Over Task does not mean choosing one versus the other. After all, Jenny would have continued her task of tidying the pavement after helping the distressed girl. POT simply allows us to focus our attention on purpose as a priority over mundane tasks when necessary. It is a practical tool that can help guide our daily steps.

But don't get me wrong, we will always need to fulfill the "tasks" in our lives. Tasks are just part of life as we know it. However, you can use POT to help you make the right choices in your life, amid the otherwise blur of tasks, to further the greater good. This can be applied in your personal life, work life, community, or anywhere else life takes you. But let's get this clear, don't go and tell your boss: "KG said I don't need to do that work. He said I should only follow my purpose!" No, that's not it at all. Putting Purpose Over Task can be a powerful tool to help when both task and purpose present themselves.

POT can permit you to act in alignment with what is most important to you, your organization, or your family. Using this tool helps you recognize purpose amongst the mundane. It's like the Baader-Meinhof phenomenon, the psychological theory behind buying a red car and then suddenly noticing red cars everywhere. Has that ever happened to you? No, there are not more red cars on the highway or in your neighborhood. There was no sale on red cars, and there is no conspiracy. No, the world did not change; your perspective did. The same applies to Purpose Over Task. Once you understand POT, you will become acutely aware of life's moments that I call "productive purpose"—those steps you take toward your purpose that become habitual and continue to contribute to the big picture.

THE TASK

Do you get buried in the task? Or are you able to pierce through the fog of the trivial to find purpose in what you do? Many of us use *tasks* as a procrastination tool. Sometimes it's that we don't understand what our purpose is yet. Other times it's because we distract ourselves from the most important things to which we should be dedicating our time. Whatever the case, the task should ultimately be treated as trivial. I know saying the word "trivial" will get me into trouble, so a less confronting definition is "trivial within the context of your other life goals."

I'm not saying that tasks are insignificant or that it is unnecessary to do some tasks in life, especially when those tasks are things that we do to pay our mortgage or put food on the table. A task can also be the things we must do to keep our home clean, tidy, and organized or the things that we have to do to feed our family. Those aren't trivial in the day-to-day sense, but when you look back at the last five or ten years of your life, are those the things that are going to matter? Are they the things that you will look back on and say, "Wow, I can't believe I did that," or "I'm so proud to be a part of that!" If not, they are likely in the category of a task.

Some tasks can and will contribute to the purpose, and that's the difference. You choose the task when it contributes to the purpose. When there is a choice, that is. Sometimes, there is no choice. The day is full of tasks; it's an unavoidable fact. That makes the choices easy. You do the job to the very best of your ability. But when given the chance, and life presents you with something aligned to your purpose, you do *that thing* first—without question! The beauty of understanding this tool is that you can now look for the difference in everything you do.

Here are a few useful examples of how POT can be applied in different situations:

- Local café: Choose to help a customer (purpose) over continuing to wipe the tables (task) when customers are waiting.
- Web designer: Deliver a feature that helps customers first (purpose) over a potential revenue-generating feature that has little customer benefit (task).
- Family time: Spend time with your family playing board games (purpose) over organizing your finances (task).
- Personal goals: Studying and taking action toward achieving your new career goals (purpose) over complaining to your peers about your current role (task).

MOONSHOT

William James said, "I will act as if what I do will make a difference." This statement ties in with the notion of Purpose Over Task and connects with a story I heard about former President John F. Kennedy (JFK) during the time the United States announced its mission to go to the moon.

During the 1960s, the United States was in the middle of the Cold War with the Soviet Union. The Soviets had recently claimed space dominance when Soviet pilot and cosmonaut Yuri Gagarin became the first human in space. JFK responded boldly by calling a special joint session of Congress in the last week of spring in 1961. It was there when JFK took the step that possibly defined his presidency, proclaiming:

> "I believe we should go to the moon. But I think every citizen of this country, as well as the members of the Congress, should consider the matter carefully in making their judgment, to which we have given attention over many weeks and months, because it is a heavy burden, and there is no sense in agreeing or desiring that the United States take an affirmative position in outer space unless we are prepared to do the work and bear the burdens to make it successful."

It was this request that made way for the Apollo program and gave the United States a singular unifying goal to put a man on the moon by the end of the decade. Notice that JFK cleverly included all of "the citizens" in his plea. With this statement, JFK was asking the whole country to commit to this mission.

After this grand declaration of the new ambition of the United States, JFK toured the country. He then famously affirmed to the American people that "We choose to go to the moon in this decade and do the other things, not because they are easy, but because they are hard because that goal will serve to organize and measure the best of our energies and skills…" It was during this tour that he first visited the facilities of NASA in Houston, Texas. This is where another classic example of Purpose Over Task was famously displayed.

While walking through the enormous facilities of the future command center of the Apollo missions, JFK and his entourage passed by a man who appeared to be part of the facilities maintenance team and was mopping the floors. Kennedy commonly connected with the workers on his tour, doing meet-and-greets along the way. But this man was steadily working and not particularly distracted by the chorus of people walking the halls. As the tour continued, Kennedy passed the man and said: "Hi, I'm Jack. What do you do for us here at NASA?" The man stopped briefly and quipped back, "I'm helping put a man on the moon, Mr. President."

The NASA maintenance man understood a different aspect of Purpose Over Task. He understood our simple human desire to be a part of something greater than ourselves. He understood that his work, however mundane, however small in the grand scheme of the thousands now working on the Apollo mission, contributed to the overall purpose—to the purpose of NASA, to the purpose of the country. To the purpose that captured the attention of humanity, culminating with the Apollo 11 mission, which landed Neil Armstrong and Buzz Aldrin on the surface of the moon on July 21, 1969. Through his attitude, actions, and words, the janitor chose to see the purpose of what he did day to day as contributing to that challenge issued to the nation over the seemingly simple task of mopping the floor.

This is the true power of POT. By using POT as a tool, you can make daily choices to consciously choose how you perceive your daily tasks. You can still align your daily tasks with a greater purpose. Whether you are the CIO of a multinational corporation or the cashier at a neighborhood grocer, you need to find your P; then, as a leader, you can teach others to find theirs. Once you understand your "Apollo mission," once you understand your "happiest place on earth," you can use that to focus your efforts on the right things. That's the ultimate use of Purpose Over Task.

USING POT DAILY

- What are my tasks for today? Am I focusing my energy on the right things?
- What is my purpose? Do I have my priorities right?
- Do my tasks align with my purpose today?
- If I had more time, could I accomplish my goals?

If you find yourself struggling with any of these questions, I highly recommend a daily dose of POT, for medicinal purposes only—just joking! Even if you don't have a handle on your life's purpose at this stage personally or within your career, practice using POT on some of the minor goals you are trying to accomplish. You may have a corporate charter that you are trying to align yourself with, or a church mission as your priority. These are all areas where you can practice the use of Purpose Over Task. And if you are thinking to yourself, *This POT stuff would be cool, but I don't know my purpose*, don't sweat it. We will cover the topic of purpose in more detail within Tool #5: Play.

Trust me. I know this is not a simple thing. Before I discovered POT, I struggled with this myself for many years, so I can't throw stones when it comes to questioning one's focus, direction, or priorities. For many years, I kept myself really, really busy doing lots of things. I was one of those people who always used the phrase, "I'm really busy," in response to the question, "How have you been?" or "What have you been up to?" whenever I ran into an acquaintance at a party. It was my standard grand answer. And, it was the truth. I was always doing something. I was always working on a side project, always helping a friend out, always learning something new. I did this for many years. I was ambitious, hopeful, and ignorant all at once. Blissfully ignorant and unaware, nonetheless. Like so many of you, I was busy doing lots of good things, but I wasn't necessarily busy doing the right things. Ask yourself, "Am I too busy?" By using POT as a mantra and a tool to cut through the noise, *purpose* will become the red car in your world. You will find it everywhere.

IN RETROSPECT

Tool #1—Use Purpose Over Task

- This tool teaches us to find meaning in our daily pursuits and use Purpose Over Task as a guidepost in our careers and personal lives.

- We learned that using Purpose Over Task (POT) as a mantra can help distill one's thinking to choose what is most important.

- As leaders, we can help others find purpose in their daily lives by aligning with a grand mission.

Practice Leading with Purpose Over Task

1. Take a moment to ask yourself or your team, "How do I fit into the mission of my company?" "How does my daily task fit into the purpose of the company?"

2. Doing things with your friends and family is better (purpose) than doing things for them (task). Take a moment to consider those whom you care for the most, and make sure you are choosing POT with your interactions.

3. Think about the people you are working with within your community. Have you become lost in the day-to-day operations? Have you forgotten the purpose? Take this opportunity to realign to your purpose as a group.

> THE MOST INTIMATE TEMPER OF A PEOPLE, ITS DEEPEST SOUL, IS ABOVE ALL IN ITS LANGUAGE.

—JULES MICHELET

TOOL #2

Learn a New Language

This tool is admittedly a little tongue-in-cheek. Spoiler alert: "Learn a New Language" is not about learning a new dialect. Although being bilingual is always a bonus in life, this is not a tool praising the benefits of knowing multiple languages in business. This is a tool about connection, empathy, and inspiration. By recognizing language as a tool, you'll achieve a better connection with your staff, community, family, and customers. But before we dive into the details of what it means to Learn a New Language, I'll tell you about my boardroom experience with the subject of Tool #2: language.

SPEAKING SWAHILI

I had been preparing for a presentation for weeks and working on the deal for months. This was a big opportunity for me both personally and professionally, since it was my first time presenting in front of the board after becoming practice manager almost three months prior. One of my mentors and manager at the time had allowed me to take the lead in this proposal to gain valuable exposure with the members of the board, and I wasn't about to mess it up. This was a high-value transformation proposal that would cost the company millions in additional license fees. It was my job to let the board of directors know why it was a suitable investment for the company's future, despite the cost.

I was ready. I knew the financial details from top to bottom, and I understood the features, benefits, and risks like the back of my hand. Being a consultant for many years, I was also able to create a visually stunning PowerPoint deck, so I expected to deliver a killer presentation. My boss and I had gone over all the information one last time before the session, so I knew my preparation would not be an issue. I was fully prepared to dazzle the executives with my knowledge and presentation skills. I was anxious but confident as I entered the room full of company executives. However, dazzled wasn't how I would describe their reactions.

We only had fifteen minutes on the agenda, so I knew the message had to be short and to the point. I started with my first slide of three in total, and I knew something was amiss. One of the things that my boss and I agreed on when preparing the slide deck was to get right to the heart of the discussion. She knew the group well and advised that they would switch off or get bored quickly unless I started with the core of the message. My first slide did precisely that. It was a brilliantly designed PowerPoint slide that had it all. The first image presented on the conference room's big-screen Panasonic television was my pitch in quartered sections. The page projected the problem, the solution, the potential risks, and mitigations all on a single page. It was solid.

The boardroom was filled with six middle-aged men and two women, one of whom was the executive assistant running the slideshow and managing the agenda. The group sat stoically in a semicircle around a modern rectangular meeting room table. As I stood at the head of the room near the TV screen, my manager took a seat in one of the empty black leather chairs at one end of the room. I started to explain the proposal, being careful to hit on all of the critical aspects of the business case. This strategy was initially met with approving nods of acknowledgment. But it was the question that came from the left side of the room that started the rapid descent of the positive energy: "But what about the sunk costs?" It was the beginning of my realization that language has layers and subtleties that need to be understood. "Sunk costs?" I said as if repeating the words would help me understand what was being asked.

"Yes, the sunk costs and the Opex. Where is that covered?" the director said, topping my unknowing query with yet another question. The noise in my head started to ring with anxiousness as I reached deep into the recesses of my mind, trying to make sense of the words. At that moment, I knew that everything being asked was in English. After all, each of the directors spoke English as their first language, but the words presented to me did not make the question understandable. My brain was not comprehending how "sunk costs" or "Opex" fit into the English language, which I have been well versed in since birth. The words might as well have been Swahili to my muddled brain.

Gracefully and graciously, my boss and mentor stepped in and began to interpret what I was attempting to say. I smiled in agreement as she intuitively hit every note on their proverbial hymn sheet. She explained how we had already addressed the "sunk cost" in the presentation section under previous expenses. She also drew their attention to the next slide that outlined the annual operating expenses to swiftly answer the open question of "Opex." She was well versed in the language of this tribe and started to explain other aspects of the presentation in the native tongue of the group. She offered information about "hard benefits," "soft benefits," "ROI," and "cost avoidance," which immediately connected with the directors.

These were phrases that continued to elude my understanding. I could only watch, listen, and learn as I became schooled in the unique vernacular of the group. But all was not lost. Ultimately, the hard work and preparation had paid off. The proposal was accepted, and I went on to have many more successful interactions with those directors. But it was through this experience, along with many others throughout my career and personal life, that highlighted the importance of Tool #2.

Learning a New Language is not simply about the fancy words or business jargon you use. In fact, it is not about buzzwords, slang, or exclusive lingo at all. By learning the language of your tribe, your team, your family, and your spouse, you can grow to experience people from a truly new perspective. Whether it's the tribe you already belong to or the one in which you seek to be indoctrinated, understanding more about the nuance of language can change how you think and connect with others.

FINDING THE WORDS

What is "language?" Language is the way we share thoughts, emotions, and ideas. It is one of the fundamentals of communication and cultural connection. Most estimates have language developing over 50,000 years ago, around the time Homo sapiens evolved, and it is considered one of the most important evolutionary threads of human existence. Language helps unite us and can equally tear us apart. It is through language that we express our intent to others. Language, or our mastery thereof, can also impact how we think as leaders, as groups, and as people. Our language can influence how we see the world.

This notion of a person's spoken language having a direct and profound impact on how that person thinks was popularized during the early twentieth century through research conducted by anthropologists Edward Sapir and Benjamin Lee Whorf. They believed that the structure of a language affects the speaker's understanding and view of the world. In other words, the speaker's perception of the world is relative to their spoken language. This theory is commonly known as the Sapir–Whorf hypothesis or linguistic relativity. So how does this work? Let's take the example of the word "snow" in the English language. Due to the inherent structure of the language, this word in English only has a singular description. Therefore, in the mind of someone who speaks English, "snow" is simply "snow," that fluffy, icy substance that falls from the sky and covers the ground at times during winter. Pretty straightforward, right? Now take that same word and compare it to the language structure of Eskimos.

According to explorer Franz Boas, Inuktitut, the Inuit Eskimo language, has many more words that all describe "snow." Boas noted that there are dozens of Inuktitut terms for "frozen precipitation." There is *aqilokoq*, which is softly fallen snow. There is *apun*, which is snow on the ground. And there is *qaneq*, which means falling snow. So on a wintry evening, while watching the snow drift to the ground, the mind of an Eskimo is wired differently. The Eskimos' perception of snow is colored by a myriad of nuances related to how the snow is falling, the effects of the wind, and every other detailed variation relative to the Inuit language. Although Sapir and Whorf's theory is squarely related to national or cultural dialects, this notion of our words and language impacting our thinking is essential, especially as leaders.

Like my experience with the boardroom presentation and the word structure of Inuktitut, language has an impact. Knowing the correct language is important. Think about planning to travel to a foreign country where they speak a different language. Before you travel, you may attempt to get yourself familiar with the local customs. You may also try to learn the most useful words and phrases for that country or culture. Upon arrival at your destination, you do your best to speak the language as authentically as possible. This allows the native people to know that you are trying to assimilate and respect their culture. If your study efforts are rewarded with an understanding of your broken but well-intended phrases, you feel accomplished and closer to that community. You start to feel more akin to the people, and they begin to feel the same towards you.

Do you know the language of those whom you work with? The language of your community? The language of your kids?

Would understanding more about their language and world help you connect with them and see the nuance of their "snow" differently? The short answer is yes. By learning the language of those around us, both our thinking and our understanding can be more aligned.

LET THE GAMES BEGIN

The benefits of learning a new language can go well beyond overseas travel. I noticed this when chatting with one of the other fathers at my son's tenth birthday party. It was a perfect day for bubble soccer as we gathered twenty kids between ages ten and eleven in our local park. If you are not familiar with bubble soccer, you can be forgiven since my wife and I only learned of it when a classmate of my son had a similar birthday party months earlier. Bubble soccer is a combination of regular soccer and the human version of bumper cars, and it's so much fun to watch. The kids run around the soccer field with large, round air bubble suits, constantly bouncing off each other, bouncing off the ground, and generally having fun. A few other parents gathered to watch the spectacle that day, and we mingled, laughed, and gasped at the kids as they scurried up and down the soccer field.

I struck up a conversation with one of the fathers named Roger, and we started with the typical pleasantries. We spoke about how rambunctious the kids were, the school policies, the NBA, and the weather. I happened to ask him what their plans were for the remainder of the day after the party.

To that, he promptly answered, "Aw, we'll be getting into the games after this. It's definitely a game day."

I chuckled. "Oh, okay, that's cool. What kinds of games? Like board games?"

"Nah," Roger replied. "You know, Xbox games. And a couple of other games on the laptop, too, like Minecraft and Clash Royale."

I was very familiar with these game titles because my son was also heavily into gaming. But I was not expecting that answer from the gray-haired father of two. But my curiosity was now piqued, and I replied.

"Okay, so do you watch the boys? Or do you get your game on too?" His sons were ten and thirteen, so my thoughts were that maybe he was an innocent bystander to their gaming. But that was not the case.

He casually replied, "Of course, I get in there and give them a run for their money. We're all quite competitive, so sometimes it ends in tears. But usually, it's a blast. You should try it with Tyson. I know he's into his games too."

"I wish I had time for games," I retorted, as I folded my arms in defense.

"Trust me. It's not about playing the games," Roger replied. "Yeah, some of them are actually fun. Some are pretty challenging for me, too, and hopefully, that's good to keep the cobwebs out of the ole brain. You know? But honestly, it's about having the chance to connect with my boys."

Suddenly, my senses were awakened. The conversation flipped from typical social small talk to a genuine learning moment for me. He continued, "My boys spent loads of time talking to each other and their friends about these games, and I just wanted to be a part of their life. I discovered their worlds of clans, towers, capturing jewels, mods, bed wars, and speed-bridging. By playing with them, I get it. I'm not just skating on the surface or watching from the sidelines. I'm no longer clueless and just repeating the names of characters that I had no idea about. Now, I not only know the names, but I also understand why it's important to my kids. I speak their language, and it's changed our relationship for the better."

What Roger does with his kids is form a shared language connection to understand the culture of his boys. It is through learning and language sharing that we build unspoken bonds and levels of trust as leaders. And no, this tool is not about simply being able to repeat or reflect the words back to others. Parroting phrases back to others is a well-known psychological ploy used by many salesmen, politicians, and leaders to influence others, but that is not learning the language. To use Tool #2 effectively, you need to immerse yourself in the language. My friend Roger understood this principle when he started gaming with his sons. Skimming the surface doesn't work. It can even work against you and lead to cynicism and distrust. Roger understood that by only having a surface-level knowledge of jargon or simply parroting back phrases out of context, he was not getting closer to his tribe. To truly learn the language of his boys, he needed to be an active participant in their world. He needed to think differently about their world. By practicing Tool #2, he was learning something new, creating new strands of trust with his kids, and developing empathy by understanding more about their gaming adventures. That's connection. That's the power of learning a new language, and that's something every leader should strive to do.

TWO-SIDED TOOL

Some tools are simple and have a singular purpose, like a screwdriver or socket wrench, while others are considered multipurpose. These multipurpose tools can be as diverse as a Swiss army knife or as simple as a hammer. The hammer consists of two tools in one. It has the hammer face for driving in a nail and the hammer claw for pulling out the nail or prying, like a crowbar. In the same way, many of the tools of 10LT will be multipurpose. This is true for Tool #2. Not only is learning a new language about connecting with others through a shared language and experience, but it is also about leading others with a new language, the language of leaders. How is this different from learning the language of the executives in the boardroom? This side of Tool #2 is not only about connecting; it is about communicating through your use of language and tone.

To help demonstrate this, do me a favor. Take a moment to write down the ten leaders that have had the most impact on you. They can be leaders from the past or present, from your faith or the football field, from the history books, or your history teacher. It can be anyone who has provided inspiration in your life.

What does your list look like?

I try to do this every year to set goals for myself. Why do I create a list of leaders while thinking about my personal goals? Because the list helps remind me of the person I aspire to be. It reminds me that how I do life is just as important as what I do in life. My list is littered with people who have inspired me in ways both large and small. It reminds me that these people have given of themselves and, knowingly or unknowingly, had a material influence on me. It reminds me that, as part of examining my own goals at any given time, I should follow in the footsteps of those on my list and be an example to others in some small way. I recommend revisiting the list you just created regularly because your list will change. I know it seems strange, but as we grow and change as people, our values and priorities change as well. Therefore, the list of people who inspire you will also vary.

My ten-leaders list has morphed and changed over the years. But my list at the time of writing this book included teachers and coaches, like my eighth-grade public speaking teacher, Mrs. Shoquist, and a couple of my old football coaches, Coach Mullins and Coach Thomas. It also included world leaders like Martin Luther King Jr. and Barack Obama. My leader list also includes people who shaped my day-to-day life, like Dan Basso, cofounder of Systemware Inc., a software company I worked for in Dallas. My list also included my mother and Aunt Gloria, who both raised me and taught me to be the man I am today. What is your list like? Why are those people on your list? Of all the people you have known, grown up with, met in passing, read about, or worked with, why are these people in your top ten? And don't worry if you struggled to think of ten, or if you couldn't narrow it down to only ten. I just wanted you to see that impactful leaders will come in all different forms, from the public arena to the most intimate. Whomever your list includes, my guess is that they are the people who inspire you through their actions, their abilities, their belief in you, or through their words of hope and encouragement. Those words could be through what they say or how they say it. The way a leader communicates, as well as their character, has a huge impact on us, and this is the other part of Tool #2 that we need to explore.

There are many different ways in which leaders inspire us through language. There is no silver bullet for inspiring others. However, over the years and after working with thousands of growing leaders, I have discovered a simple tool that can help anyone start to speak the language of leaders. I like to call this tool of modern leaders "GIO." GIO can be used to remind us of ways to adjust how we communicate with others using the techniques of the greatest leaders through our language of gratitude, interdependence, and optimism.

GRATITUDE, INTERDEPENDENCE, AND OPTIMISM: GIO

Our words matter, whether speaking to Little League baseball parents or blogging about your favorite recipe. Our language does not require a speechwriter or a particular level of eloquence; however, the best leaders understand that their tone, their language, and their words make a difference. Especially when we are hoping to lead, influence, or even inspire others. As a parent, tone matters when raising children. As an environmental activist, language matters when encouraging others to join a cause. As a new supervisor at a department store, words matter while striving to earn the respect of new team members. As leaders, we desire to have our words and tone reflect our intent, our purpose, and the things we want others to emulate. That's just what leaders do. We will talk about this notion of having others follow us in Tool #4, but here is where we start to mold our language to fit who we are or who we want to be. Although there is no secret formula or magic wand when it comes to having the right words of inspiration, tuning your language to reflect a tone of GIO can be a great place to start.

IT STARTS WITH GRATITUDE

Thank you! *Merci*! *Grazie*! (*Domo*) *Arigato*! *Do jeh*! *Spasiba*! *Mahalo*! No matter your native language or culture, we all want to be appreciated. As human beings, we are all wired to experience positive emotions when someone expresses gratitude toward us. Studies show that we trust more, we connect more, and we work harder for those who appreciate our work. So as a leader, expressing genuine gratitude can have a significant impact on how others view you. A study by a group at the Wharton School of the University of Pennsylvania demonstrated this impact. Researchers looked at a team of university fundraisers and randomly divided them into two groups. The first group immediately went to work making phone calls to solicit alumni donations in the same way they always had. The second group of fundraisers, prior to starting, were told by a leader that she was grateful for their efforts. After reviewing the results the following week, the fundraising staff who heard the message of gratitude made 50 percent more calls than those who didn't receive that small sentiment of gratitude. That's a significant impact for a seemingly simple action.

Gratitude is defined as the quality of being thankful. It is a willingness to show appreciation for something or someone, including an appropriate amount of sincere appreciation in your conversations with your son, daughter, spouse, or unproductive staffer. Gratitude always makes a significant difference. I know for me personally, I do more for those who appreciate my work, acknowledge my efforts, or see value in the action I've put in. And I'm betting the same applies to most of you reading this book. Saying "thank you" reminds people that what they do is important. I know some of you are thinking to yourself, *KG, I'm all good on this one. I was raised right and say thank you all the time. Tick.* If this is you, that's great, but I have a challenge for you that will take your gratitude to the next level. The next time you show appreciation with the words "thank you," try to make it intentional. Try to make your "thank you" or the gesture of gratitude the center of your conversation. This can be hard work, trust me. In Western cultures, and within many other languages and cultures, we often say words like "thank you" or "thanks" as a part of everyday conversation. Growing up in Texas and being raised as a good Southern gentleman, I said these words all the time. "Cool, thanks!" or "Got it, thanks!" or "No, thank you!" and many other variations. Yes, I was saying the words. Yes, I really meant it. But that was me being polite, not appreciative. Random thank-yous do not show gratitude. There is a difference.

The next time you want to truly show appreciation or gratitude, make a thank-you statement with intentionality. The best way to show our intentions is by ensuring that there is no qualifying statement before or after the words "thank you." We also need to make sure that the words stand alone versus being intermingled amongst your many other thoughts.

Change your language from, "Thanks for that, but can you finish the other one by the end of the day?" to a simple, "That was really good. Thank you!" That's it. Having the appreciation be the last part of your statement or having a deliberate pause can be especially effective. Try saying thank you with a deliberate pause of three to five seconds afterward. Try it; it's harder than you think. It's hard not to add filler words, hidden requests, or backhanded compliments to our normal conversational attempts at appreciation. A good test is if it feels a bit awkward and uncomfortable without transitioning to creepy, you've done it right. Remember, the most important element of gratitude is sincerity.

"WE" ARE THE "FUTURE"

Now let's talk about the IO portion of the leaders' language tool GIO: interdependence and optimism. We now understand the power and potential of gratitude (the G), so let's explore the language superpowers of interdependence and optimism. Interdependence is the state or quality of being mutually dependent on each other. Whether it's a romantic relationship, a sports team, or a corporate setting, an interdependent connection implies a reliance on the individual or group. When it comes to the language of interdependence, the simplest way to think of it is "we talk." The use of interdependent or inclusive language like "we" or "us" tells the listener, "We are in this together." Have a read of this excerpt from the great orator Winston Churchill as an example:

"Even though large tracts of Europe and many old and famous States have fallen or may fall into the grip of the Gestapo and all the odious apparatus of Nazi rule, we shall not flag or fail. We shall go on to the end, we shall fight in France, we shall fight on the seas and oceans, we shall fight with growing confidence and growing strength in the air, we shall defend our Island, whatever the cost may be, we shall fight on the beaches, we shall fight on the landing grounds, we shall fight in the fields and in the streets, we shall fight in the hills; we shall never surrender, and even if, which I do not for a moment believe, this Island or a large part of it were subjugated and starving, then our Empire beyond the seas, armed and guarded by the British Fleet, would carry on the struggle, until, in God's good time, the New World, with all its power and might, steps forth to the rescue and the liberation of the old."

This speech was one of Churchill's most inspiring talks to the British House of Commons after a battle of the French port of Dunkirk during the Second World War. Did you notice the "we talk?" Did you notice the deliberate use of language that gives every Brit, every reader, every listener the sense of inclusion or even mutual obligation to succeed? "*We* shall not flag... *We* shall fight... *our* Empire beyond the seas."

The use of interdependent language can be powerful in any situation, including your team or in your home. A recent study led by Psychologist Megan Robbins of the University of California Riverside helps confirm this thinking. Robbins and her team reviewed and analyzed thirty studies of more than five thousand participants and concluded that a subtle shift in our language from self-oriented to relationship-oriented could be a predictor of relationship success. There is some debate on whether relationship-oriented talk leads to better relationships, or if better relationships lead to relationship-oriented talk (it's the classic chicken-and-egg debate). But there is no debate that this simple language shift can positively impact the thinking and perception within the relationship, and that is precisely the type of impact we seek as leaders. Our language can be a powerful tool in how we connect with others.

The use of inclusive pronouns is not the only language tool used by Churchill in his famous speech above. Take a moment to re-read the excerpt, and this time, take note of the use of the O in GIO: *optimism*. Notice Churchill's use of expressions like "we shall" and "with growing confidence and growing strength." In this way, he is injecting a sense of hope for things to come. Optimism is defined as a sense or feeling of confidence and hopefulness about the future or success to come.

Yes, learning a new language can also show off your future thinking skills and, more importantly, how you as a leader can reflect optimism for those around you. When I say "optimism," I realize that some of you are thinking about those annoying people who are super-positive and sickly sweet with happiness. No, that is just irritating, not optimistic. Think of optimism as the glass-half-full analogy—measured but with a positive view. Some of you might protest: "I'm a realist, KG, so this optimism stuff is just not for me." Well, let me help reframe your view of optimism. As part of GIO, optimism means taking in the challenges of today for what they are while also having a sense of hope that there is a future better than today. In essence, being optimistic means being a realist but not getting stuck in the mire of the moment. The optimist has the sense that no matter today's difficulty, the outlook for the future is better; tomorrow, the sun will rise, and the clouds will pass. You can call it belief or faith, but the feeling is the same no matter the term used. The best leaders, the most influential leaders, and the ones who have the most significant impact are the ones who provide a realistic sense that the future is better than today. Through their words or their actions, they help us feel renewed. By learning a new language, you'll discover your ability to impact the world around you. Begin using your words to make a positive impact on someone you know. In the words of Ralph Waldo Emerson, "Thought is the blossom; language the bud; action the fruit behind it."

IN RETROSPECT

Tool #2—Learn a New Language

- This tool allows us to better communicate and connect to others and see the world differently through a common language.
- Adjusting our language can also change how we think about the world around us.
- We learned how to use Gratitude, Interdependence, and Optimism (GIO) as part of our language as leaders.

Practice Leading by Learning a New Language

1. Test yourself this week as you communicate with customers or internal teams. Take note of the way you talk to them. Do you speak in their language? Or are you always expecting them to understand your language, your fee structures, and your jargon? At the end of the week, evaluate the results. Then, commit to immersing yourself in their world long enough to learn their language so you can truly connect with them.

2. Are you skating on the surface with your partner or other members of your family? Take the time to get into the details of their world. Learn the words and ways that make them tick.

3. Are you using the language of leaders when speaking to those in your community? Try to talk using some aspects of GIO in your next group setting.

> THE STORIES WE TELL MAKE THE WORLD. IF YOU WANT TO CHANGE THE WORLD, YOU NEED TO CHANGE YOUR STORY. THIS TRUTH APPLIES BOTH TO INDIVIDUALS AND INSTITUTIONS.
>
> —MICHAEL MARGOLIS

TOOL #3

Tell Different Stories

ABOUT STORIES

You can spend time trying to make people remember what you say, or you can make what you say memorable. Tool #3, Tell Different Stories, is about helping the words we utter and receive become memorable. Stories help turn our language into a storyline that can last a lifetime. So what is a story? In simple terms, a story is a narrative of interconnected life events told through words, symbols, or actions. These words help create imagery that is associated with those words. This mental imagery invokes emotion, creates amusement, allows for empathy, or sparks imagination. Unlike merely providing information, telling a story helps us compress and connect that data into neurologically significant events. Stories help take the thousands of words that we hear and the knowledge we take in and convert them into a package that the human brain self-determines as worth retaining. Stories help what we say or do become memorable.

What's the difference between plain ole information sharing and a story? Take a look at the example below of aviation legend Wiley Post.

AROUND THE WORLD IN EIGHT DAYS

The Information: Post was born in 1898 and was considered one of the world's most accomplished pilots, famous for his record-setting, round-the-world flight in eight days, fifteen hours, and fifty-one minutes.

The Story: Born in November of 1898 to a hard-working family of cotton farmers, Wiley Post spent his youth bouncing between small towns in Texas and Oklahoma before settling in Maysville, Oklahoma, in 1920. Post did not do particularly well in school but was always fascinated with mechanical devices and loved tinkering with machinery. He left home at the tender age of eleven to become a traveling repairman in a bold bid to make a better life for himself. But it was a moment in 1913, at the age of fifteen, while visiting the Lawson County Fair, when Post saw an airplane up close for the first time that changed his life forever. His destiny and desire to become a pilot were set into motion.

By 1921, after spending several years working in the Oklahoma oil fields, Post fell on hard times. Local jobs had dried up, and so did Post's hopes for a better life. Feeling desperate, Post resorted to the unthinkable. He attempted to steal a car near Grady County, Oklahoma, but was caught, arrested, and sentenced to ten years in jail. The once hopeful and ambitious Post had hit rock bottom. Post withdrew and became increasingly mentally unwell. But in a sudden turn of fortune, Post was miraculously released on parole after only thirteen months in the state facility.

Post had seen the light and continued his quest for a better life. After his release from jail, Post held many odd jobs, including one as part of the Burrell Tibbs Flying Circus as a parachute jumper. This is where he was secretly taught to fly by one of the circus pilots. Post eventually returned to work in the Oklahoma oil fields with a renewed determination to work hard and do big things. But once again, he faced an incredible challenge when he lost his left eye in an oil rig accident in 1926. Initially devastated by his apparent misfortune, the partially blind Post continued to believe in his dream. His faith and determination were rewarded.

Post's fortunes again changed for the better after receiving a compensation settlement from the oil rig accident that allowed him to buy his first airplane. Through Post's hard work and love for flight, he began breaking records in the world of aviation, winning a race across the country between Chicago and Los Angeles in 1930. By 1931, he was a household name after completing an around-the-world flight with Australian navigator Harold Gatty. Their record-setting trip took them from Roosevelt Field in New York across to Newfoundland, then to England, Germany, Russia, Alaska, Canada, and ultimately back to New York. The pair officially completed their 15,000 mile around-the-world trip in eight days, fifteen hours, and fifty-one minutes. Wiley Post, the former convict with a sixth-grade education and one eye, was now the most famous person in aviation, receiving an invitation to the White House, along with a ticker-tape parade in New York City.

Post's love of flying and curiosity also led him to pioneer the use of new aviation technologies, like autopilot and the radio compass. But Post wanted more. Through Post's experience breaking aviation records, he knew that the secret to flying faster and farther was soaring at higher altitudes. But the required technology did not exist to allow sustained high-altitude flight, at least not yet. Again, showing his resolve and affinity for tinkering, he solved this by developing the first pressurized flight suit. It was after developing this pressurized suit that he was able to fly a plane up to 50,000 feet into the stratosphere to be the first to discover a narrow stream of wind that propelled him faster and farther than anything he had ever seen. This current of wind would later be known as the jet stream. Post achieved many more aviation accolades that put his achievements in line with other aviation greats like Amelia Earhart and Charles Lindbergh. However, Post died tragically on August 15, 1935, at age thirty-six, in a plane crash with his friend and entertainment legend, Will Rogers, in Alaska.

What do you know about Wiley Post? Do you see the difference between Post's "story" and the "information" about Post? Telling you the story of Wiley Post, although it was long and detailed in some areas, allowed you to connect with Post as a person. You can't connect with simple facts in the same way. Even if you have no interest in flying planes or the world of aviation, my guess is that you were able to connect with Post's personal story on some level. Maybe it's because he was able to overcome incredible odds to achieve his dreams? Maybe because his life had its share of ups and downs like all of us? Maybe it's because of a unique connection, such as you come from Oklahoma, too, or maybe your grandfather was also a pilot? No matter what created the connection, you can begin to see that through sharing our life stories, the way we communicate becomes more effective and more meaningful.

WHY ARE STORIES GREAT TOOLS?

As people, we are wired to communicate through stories. Our society is built around storytelling mediums, whether it's through podcasts or television shows or radio or the music that we love so much. Much of what we do is captured in stories. We like hearing and reading stories because they create a feeling of emotion and memory that we can hold on to. That is partly because our brains are wired for stories and storytelling. Our brains are chemically changed when exposed to a good story. According to the research of Dr. Paul J. Zak of the Center for Neuroeconomics Studies at Claremont Graduate University, a good story is one that contains two distinct parts. First, the story must grab and hold our attention. This is usually done by creating drama through conflict or some other way of capturing the audience's attention. Second, a good story has the ability to transport its audience to be there with the character in the scene.

This simply means that the reader, viewer, or listener has to connect with the story's content enough to imagine themselves as a part of the story. In the example of Wiley Post, we do this because, as an audience, we can imagine ourselves going through similar struggles, or maybe we just love tinkering with mechanical things. This transportation of the audience causes emotional resonance with the story or the characters in the story, which releases oxytocin in the brain. Oxytocin creates feelings of empathy, trust, and connectedness. This chemical reaction changes how we feel and the way we learn. Stories that capture our attention can also produce a chemical called cortisol. In our brains, cortisol is often associated with distress. Although we are not necessarily in any distress, this chemical reaction puts our brains on high alert. It is through this heightened activity in the brain that those stories allow us to retain much more information than we would by simply stating facts. Through emotion and attention, a story becomes stickier to our brains.

Why is this important to you as a person or as a leader? Let's revisit the elements of modern leaders—connection, communication, curiosity, commitment, and context. Tell Different Stories is one of the few tools that can activate every element. A good story is not only a great communication tool that promotes connection with one another; a good story keeps us intrigued and curious. Like our story about Wiley Post, it provides a window into our character's life, providing the context we need to connect with the character and the story. It also turns out that a good story can lead to commitment or taking action. Dr. Zak and his team discovered this in an experiment funded by the Defense Advanced Research Projects Agency, DARPA. In this experiment, the research team was able to predict who would donate money with up to 80 percent accuracy based on the story they watched in a video. The researchers showed the participants one of two videos in the lab before participants were asked to make a donation. One video was the story of a father, his dying son, and their struggle to make the most of every day. The second video was used as a control and was not a proper story. It simply showed a father and son walking to the zoo. That's it. Dr. Zak and the research team noticed an overwhelming difference. The video that contained elements of a story, allowing participants to empathize with the father and son, was more likely to raise money for the designated charity. However, the video that did not arouse the viewers' curiosity or empathy but was more informational had the opposite effect, and the participants donated less.

What does Tool #3, Tell Different Stories, really mean? How can it help my family or help me become a better leader? For more than 30,000 years, humans have been storytelling. From the early murals fashioned from colored pigment found on cave walls to the stories of Greek mythology passed down through the centuries, stories have been a part of our social fabric. Tales, stories, and fables are fundamental to the way we communicate with each other by expressing our history, sharing our feelings, dreams, disappointments, and reshaping everything around us. As leaders, we can harness the incredible power of stories and use them as one of the most effective communication tools ever created. It's time to tell your story.

YOUR STORY

When you consider applying Tool #3 in your world, the key is not to think about what your story means to you. The key is to think about what it could mean to others. This perspective of *others* is crucial to choosing the story that will resonate with your listener, reader, coworker, or teammate. Think about it. You already know your own story. In fact, you probably know it all too well. So now, as you choose to share with others, you almost need to turn off your inner dialogue and start thinking about those around you. It's about making yourself one notch more vulnerable than you were before. It's about sharing a side of you that may not have been readily accessible. It's about you being open to being open.

I know some of you are on the fence with this one. You're thinking, *Wow, that's tough. I'm not sure I can do that.* Yes, you bet it's tough. It's still tough for me. But it's something we must do if we want to truly connect with other people. Some of you may be thinking the same thing that held me back for years. *Is my story interesting enough?* Or, on the opposite end of the spectrum: *My story is too embarrassing, shameful, or too confronting.* Trust me. I have thought of all of these things, too, but don't fear. Next, we'll explore how to get over these fears to get the best out of Tool #3.

IT STARTS BY STARTING FROM THE BEGINNING

We spend much of our existence today enthralled in stories. There are the overt stories we experience through media outlets like newspapers, magazines, television, and movies. We are constantly consuming these stories, whether we realize it or not. Thanks to the rise of social media, we also tell stories as they happen in real-time via Facebook, YouTube, and other similar outlets. We carefully curate our social media story, showing our followers the best of us and only what is perceived to be interesting. These are the stories that we readily share. But what we are talking about as part of Tool #3 are the stories that go beyond the headlines to illuminate your authentic story.

Some of you might be wondering, "KG, how do I create or understand my own story?" An exercise you can do is to take the time to create your own stories. I say "stories" as plural because I believe we each have many stories. Some of them will be helpful to different audiences. Some of our stories will be relevant today; others will have a purpose later. Some of them may only be helpful to us personally, allowing us to discover more of ourselves than we ever thought possible. The best way to start collecting your stories is by journaling, typing them into your computer, speaking them into your mobile phone's recorder, or any other method to capture your thoughts.

Take another break from this book and make a small journal entry, note, or short recording that describes your story. It doesn't matter how many words or if it's long or short. The key is to start capturing your thoughts. I suggest you start with the big picture, like a Wiley Post type story. I call this your origin story. These origin stories are great since they can be organized in a basic chronological fashion.

OUR ORIGIN STORY

Origin stories have been popular as of late, especially in the Marvel Universe. They tell the previously unknown background stories of comic book heroes. At the very least, we all have an origin story to tell. And stories don't have to be about extraordinary things, good over evil, or rags to riches. The purpose of a story is to set a scene, provide context, communicate, and connect. To start creating your origin story, ask yourself, "How did I get here?" We often overlook this question since it's easy to try to look at the extraordinary. However, our humble beginnings can be a great starting point for uncovering the often-hidden interesting bits of our story. Again, if you haven't done this yet, then hit pause, put down the device, place the bookmark on the page, or simply fold back the corner of the book like I usually do. Whatever literary medium you use, take a break from it to start writing down your story now. Don't worry. I'll be here when you get back!

If you are like me, the exercise of writing about yourself can be a challenge. I know it can force you to confront difficult issues and past events. If you can persevere through the awkwardness, you will start to see the narrative emerge. You will see the ups and downs in your life and eventually begin to understand your story.

Once you have your story recorded or written down, the next step is to look at the parts of your story through the eyes of other people. Look at your origin story and take note of the sections that could help others. You can put a star beside these paragraphs (or make a list on paper if you recorded them) to remind you of their importance. There will be many areas of your story that will be helpful to others. Here are a few simple suggestions on what to look for:

- A difficult situation and how you overcame it
- A funny moment that helped you think differently
- A mentor or moment that changed your direction
- The lucky break that paved the way for something new
- The bad time that ultimately led to a positive outcome
- The misfortune you endured in which you are still searching for answers

- The steady work that resulted in significant progress

DIFFERENT IS GOOD

What was your story like? Was that a hard thing to do? Or was it liberating? How is your story different from those around you? As you tell your personal story, know that being different is an integral part of what sets you apart from others. I know this because I spent many years trying to fit in with the world around me. Growing up, I was one of a handful of African American kids in my school. So my differences were on show every day. My instinct as a young boy was to try everything possible to minimize the appearance of other differences. I just wanted to fit in.

Now, as an adult, I know that fitting in does not make me interesting. Instead, the very things that make me different make my story special. My odd bits and traits make me who I am. The same applies to storytelling. It's like Wiley Post's sixth-grade education or losing an eye during an oil rig accident. These parts of Post's life are unique but help make him human. These same flaws make us all vulnerable yet accessible. Different is good. Like me, I'm guessing you have tried and failed at many things in your life. Or maybe you had a part of your life that, in many ways, you want to forget. I can relate.

But it's these imperfections, these less-than-shining moments, these human frailties that provide a genuine connection to those around us. No, I'm not recommending going out and spewing your personal life everywhere. That's not what I'm saying at all. Don't say, "KG said I should tell my story," then start gushing your life story at inappropriate times. This could quickly get awkward and downright strange if done without restraint.

However, I am saying it's perfectly fine to be vulnerable and share something personal when it can make a difference in someone else's life. In fact, as a leader, you should be more vulnerable than not. This means telling your story in parts where they are contextually appropriate and can also help others. In other words, the timing and situation are important, but be prepared and willing to share. The simple rules for new leaders when trying to share your story with others should be to keep it simple, keep it real, and make it relevant.

The real power in telling stories is that it creates the context for the people you are trying to inspire. It creates the context for yourself at the same time. One of the things that I have found most interesting about training other people on various leadership approaches is that often I get more out of it than anyone else. Inevitably, as I was trying to articulate the information, the answer became more and more clear to me at the same time. In other words, I became my own student. The focus on how to convey the message to my audience made my brain focus on its articulation. In turn, it provided a personal context as well as the ability to better communicate the message to others. This is why telling your own story becomes even more important. It not only helps others but provides the proverbial chicken soup for the soul that can promote personal clarity, reconciliation, and healing.

Remember, the stories we share are not only about us. Our shared life story is about using this tool as an opportunity to connect or communicate. So naturally, it's also about understanding the stories of others. It's about learning their context. It's also about seeing those who are close to you in new ways. Yes, Tool #3, Tell Different Stories, is as much about understanding different stories as it is about discovering our own. It's about attracting different stories in our world to truly complete our own. What does this mean? It means that as leaders, we have to hear different voices. We need to see, hear, and experience different perspectives and connect with different worlds to understand more about the world around us. Being a leader is about expanding your world, expanding your knowledge, and expanding what you consider to be true. That's what hearing and experiencing different stories can do for us.

The Bible is one of the most widely read and told collections of stories of all time. The biblical stories are told in the form of hymns, prayers, proverbs, parables, poetry, and prophecies, and many of its stories center on the life of Jesus of Nazareth. But even the Bible, as it tells the story of Jesus, uses the stories of many others to truly capture its teachings. If we look at the Bible in its entirety, some accounts show over two thousand other characters being mentioned through its tales and parables. Characters young and old, men and women, good and evil—they all contribute to the narrative of its writers. In the same way, Tool #3 is not complete if we haven't taken the opportunity as leaders to understand the stories of others.

We must take the time to understand and retell those stories in a meaningful way and provide context and platforms for others to have their stories heard. Remember, the power of stories works both ways. We want to tell stories in order to make connections, right? Therefore we should be listening and empathizing with the people around us to make similar connections. Ask yourself, "Do I know the story of the people on my team? Do I know the story of my boss? Do I know the story of those in my family?" No, I'm not talking about the surface-level stuff that we could glean from social media. Do you really know the story of the people you live, work, and interact with? Test yourself on this for a moment.

Make a list of your closest friends or colleagues, and try to articulate their stories in eight to ten sentences. This exercise is beneficial to understand and recognize where your relationship with others is less than optimal when it comes to knowing them deeply. How did you do? Yes, we can all write one sentence. For example, "Byron grew up in College Station, Texas, and is a great musician." But that's just the surface level. Do you know anything else about Byron? Do you know his world beyond his stats: three children, two dogs, one wife, now living in Austin? Yes, those are personal stats, but they are not Byron's story. What are Byron's greatest dreams? Who does he admire? What are Byron's fears and motivations? These are the different stories we need to uncover to help fully understand who we work with or why Byron is the way he is. Others' stories help us step deeper into our own.

As leaders, we need to think of ourselves as reporters, looking for those nuggets of gold in the form of someone's story, then bringing them to the forefront for others to see or hear. Now, I know that it sounds like I'm saying to "expose" the stories of others. But that's not exactly true. I only want you to retell someone's story if they give you express permission to do so. Someone else's story should be considered sacred and shared only by that person when they are ready. What do you do if you find a great story, but it's too personal, or the person does not want you to share it? What I have learned over time is that we can tell the stories of others through many mechanisms. Sometimes we can help tell the great stories of those around us through our language or words. Other times, we tell those different stories by providing opportunities or platforms. We provide an opportunity for others to experience new things or an opportunity for others to see or hear a different perspective.

I find that adding new faces and voices to an already established group is a great way to Tell Different Stories. I once worked with a team that had been together for over five years. A colleague hired a person named Chuck, who was neurodivergent, to join our well-established team. Neurodivergence applies to anyone who has cognitive challenges, such as autism, ADHD, and learning disabilities such as dyslexia. As a team, we had never considered ourselves uninformed, ignorant, or discriminatory, but suddenly being exposed to someone with different thinking and challenges to ours changed how we functioned as a group. We became more aware of and responsive to those with neurological and other challenges that we once took for granted. I cannot remember hearing any details about Chuck's condition, but by having the opportunity to work alongside Chuck, our perspective was changed. That's not literally telling Chuck's biography as we would traditionally tell a story, but it can be one of the most powerful ways to introduce and expose people to new views, which ultimately is the story. So tell the story of the quiet person on your team, the elusive neighbor, or the disabled vet who needs your help. Tell your story while revealing the characters in the stories around you. That's what Tool #3 is all about.

I know this tool will excite some of you and completely terrify others, and that's okay. Remember, use the tools that you want when you want them. The most important thing is to remember that the tool is there for you when the time is right. The tool is now yours. Don't use the heel of an old shoe to finish off that nail in a plank when a shiny hammer is there and available to be used with efficiency and effectiveness.

IN RETROSPECT

Tool #3—Tell Different Stories

- This tool is about discovery and diversity. It is about finding your personal story and celebrating the stories of those around you.
- We learned that through our stories, what we say becomes more memorable since stories create neurologically significant information for the brains of our listeners.
- We learned how to create our stories by starting with our origin story.
- We can tell the stories of others in many ways, including opportunities.

Practice Leading by Telling Different Stories

1. Tell Different Stories by being a champion for diversity in your team. Be intentional in your next meeting by asking for the opinions of those without a voice.
2. Take a moment to ask your parents, siblings, or best friend this question: "What is the one thing I don't know about your childhood?" You'll be surprised at how much you didn't know.
3. Open up to your team or community group by sharing details about your background so they can understand you better. Share how you got from point A to point B; it will help inspire them.

> DO NOT FOLLOW WHERE THE PATH MAY LEAD. GO INSTEAD WHERE THERE IS NO PATH AND LEAVE A TRAIL.
>
> —MURIEL STRODE

TOOL #4

Create Currents

"**M**-I-L-I-E-U," young Balu slowly spelled out.
"That is correct!" proclaimed the moderator.

And with that, Balu Natarajan correctly spelled the final word needed to be crowned the champion of the 1985 Scripps National Spelling Bee held in Washington, DC. He stepped back to embrace the moment amongst a sea of flashing lights. This was an incredible accomplishment for the thirteen-year-old. It was even more incredible knowing that Natarajan was the son of immigrant parents who migrated from India only fifteen years prior and still spoke their native Tamil at home. It was Natarajan's third attempt at the annual national competition, this time outlasting 167 other regional winners. This was certainly Natarajan's day. But little did the eighth-grader know that his hours of hard work and study would transcend mere personal achievement. This summer night in June began something extraordinary in the world of America's most prestigious spelling bee forever. Balu Natarajan Created a Current.

The E. W. Scripps Company began sponsoring the Scripps National Spelling Bee in the 1920s and has been a North American tradition for over one hundred years. But something happened after Natarajan's historic win in 1985 that can only be explained as phenomenal. The first glimpse of the phenomenon occurred three short years later when Rageshree Ramachandran became the Scripps National Spelling Bee champion in 1988. Ramachandran beat a record two hundred contestants by correctly spelling the word "elegiacal." Like Natarajan before her, Ramachandran was thirteen years old when she was able to hoist the trophy for the Superbowl of spelling bees. And also, like Natarajan, Ramachandran is of Indian descent. Both of these similarities would normally be considered an interesting coincidence, but when we fast-forward three decades later to 2018, a surprising pattern started to emerge. By 2018, the *current* that started as a trickle of hope for other Indian-American kids and their parents had turned into a tidal wave of dominance. By the time Karthik Nemmani stood on stage as the winner in the ninety-third year of the Scripps National Spelling Bee, he was the fourteenth South Asian winner or co-winner in eleven consecutive years. As a first-time national spelling bee contestant, fourteen-year-old Nemmani may not have realized that his path to glory was ignited more than thirty years before.

The question is, why? How does this happen? What caused this tsunami of Indian-American dominance in the world of the spelling bee? Is it genetics? Is it the spelling-bee-obsessed parents? Is it simply that these kids work harder than other kids? The answer is likely a combination of factors. One factor is the namesake of Tool #4, a little-known phenomenon that I call Create Currents.

WHAT ARE CURRENTS?

We know currents exist in nature in many forms. From the sea currents responsible for the regulation of temperature in Earth's oceans to the powerful airborne currents like the jet stream Wiley Post discovered high above the globe. Currents are all around us. A current is loosely defined as "moving air or fluid passing through a slower body of water or air." Another definition considers the electricity that powers our household appliances, defining the current as "a directional movement of positively charged particles." But these are not the currents that Tool #4 represents. Tool #4 is not about oceans or electricity. But if you can visualize the inner workings of these physical currents, you will start to get a glimpse of the power behind Tool #4. Creating Currents is about ideological waves that move amongst and between people—and ultimately influence people!

The idea of currents as a human-generated force was first introduced in the late 1800s by one of the fathers of modern sociology, Emile Durkheim. Durkheim coined the term *social currents* when describing the impact of the conscious collective. He believed in the idea that some experiences, emotions, and actions go beyond an individual's perspective and are influenced by other forces. This type of consciousness within society is only activated when being exposed to others in a group context—collective consciousness. It is in the collective that people act in extraordinary ways that would not be possible as an individual. Historic examples could include events like the Reign of Terror as part of the French Revolution, the LA riots of 1992 or 2020, or the spate of UFO sightings in New Mexico. These events all led people to believe or act differently when exposed to the group or collective.

Durkheim believed that social currents, unlike other social facts, were coercive to individuals and had the ability to directly impact a person's belief system. This sounds extraordinary since a person's beliefs are often integral to the very definition of that person and who they are. What we believe is at the heart of our very identity. Our beliefs govern our moral compass, our personality, our choices in a partner, and often help determine our path in life. So altering one's beliefs could be considered life-changing—whether positive or negative. But what Durkheim observed was that certain social influences have such a powerful impact on individuals that what was once considered morally wrong in the past (or only moments ago) could now be considered acceptable. In the same way, through the influence of others, things that seemed impossible yesterday could suddenly be deemed possible today. Although Durkheim's assessment of social currents was primarily based on observing significant social events and movements, these currents exist in our day-to-day lives. Currents are also created in the microcosm of our world, and I call these forces *local currents*. These local currents can be equally powerful in their pull on social situations and our immediate circle of influence but are generated by individuals, or a small cohort, unlike social currents.

How does this sociological theory of human forces relate to the dominance of the Indian-American students in the national spelling bee? In 1985, the belief system of many Indian-Americans changed. It was brave children like Balu Natarajan who led the way. For many sons and daughters of immigrants, that

Thursday afternoon on June the 6th, a current was created by Natarajan. The impossible became possible.

Let's look at another example that can help us to further understand how we Create Currents for others by leading the way. On May 6, 1954, a young British athlete beat his personal best (PB) middle-distance running time by just over 2 seconds. In many prior attempts, the best time he could muster was 4 minutes and 2 seconds, which still happened to be one of the fastest in the world. When Roger Bannister ran his PB in the one-mile event in 3 minutes 59.4 seconds, Bannister became the first person in history to accomplish the mythical "4-minute mile." Although only under 4 minutes by milliseconds, this was a milestone that had been chased for decades by middle-distance runners but had seemed all but impossible until that day.

But much like Natarajan's spelling bee win, Bannister's moment of glory started a wave of change in the sport of running forever. In fact, within a mere forty-six days, Bannister's record was surpassed by his Australian rival, John Landy, when Landy completed the mile in 3 minutes 58 seconds. And with Bannister and Landy doing what had been impossible for decades, a year later, three runners shattered the 4-minute barrier within a single race. Yes, what had not been possible for decades was now becoming commonplace.

Think about it. Bannister's run, although ultimately considered extraordinary, was only 2 seconds different from his prior attempts and only under that magical 4-minute mark by a few tenths of a second. Yes, tenths of a second. In most situations, 6-tenths of a second may be questioned as a "margin of error," but it was those milliseconds that made all the difference.

The current was sparked. Now, the beliefs of the collective had changed. Belief had not only changed for Bannister and other runners; it had also changed for the coaches. It changed for the reporters and promoters and anyone else who was connected to the sport of running. Now the notion of what was considered achievable had changed, not slowly or over time, but almost in an instant. Bannister was able to Create a Current that would continue for the next half-century. The sub-4-minute mile has now become the standard for elite middle-distance runners all over the world.

Tool #4, Create Currents, is about creating a pathway for others. As leaders, this is especially important, knowing that you are leading the way by your actions. It's important to know that your actions matter. One of my good friends, Gerard Davis, always says that we should use our superpowers for good; indeed, Creating Currents is an outward display of using our superpowers for good. The key to Creating Currents as a form of leadership is to remember that someone is following you no matter where you start from. Your role then becomes to understand how leading yourself serves to clear the path for others.

Even while writing this book, invisible currents were at play, and a pathway was created for me. It was only through discovering that Jason, one of my professional connections, wrote a book, which then made me consider writing a book. Before this random discovery of information during a dinner conversation with my wife, writing a book simply wasn't something that regular people did—at least in my mind. Reading books seemed perfectly normal, but only super brainy academics or literary wizards wrote books, right? I did not know Jason well, but in all of our prior contacts, he seemed like a normal guy. He seemed smart and knowledgeable about real estate investments; otherwise, he wasn't some sort of super-elite academic whom I couldn't relate to. And he did it. Jason wrote a book. That was the first inkling of my wild internal dialog. *Maybe I can write a book. Maybe it's not unattainable.*

As interesting as the idea was, that thought faded with the digestion of my meal that evening. Then a few months later, the current resurfaced. A former colleague whom I worked with briefly at one of the prominent financial services companies in Australia posted a note on the business social media site, LinkedIn. The post from Phillimon Zongo read, "I have finished my first book." That was it. Again, Phillimon was a regular guy. But Phillimon was also a man of color, like me. He was a father, like me. And he was a technologist, like me. That single line in a social media post gave me a new belief and a push, which I attribute to the current being activated. I now had a new belief in what was possible; my bubble of belief had expanded. Both Jason and Phillimon Created Currents, and it was through these currents that *10 Leading Tools* (10LT) was born.

BIRDS OF A FEATHER

There's a certain mystic beauty to the way birds fly with meticulous freedom. I watch in awe as they soar to dizzying heights with such grace, such precision, such responsiveness, and with such trust. They have a magical relationship with the sky that has long fueled many childhood dreams. By watching the movement of birds, one can glean how nature uses the currents on many levels.

The signature pattern of migratory birds is so familiar; the clever V-shaped formation is a skyward symbol of commitment, connection, and unity. This symmetric pattern is a common sight amongst ducks, geese, swans, and other birds known for seasonal migration. But have you ever considered why they form a V? It's probably not something you think about every day, but it certainly is for people like Austrian biologist Johannes Fritz, according to an article from National Geographic.

In the 2014 article, Fritz and his team of Austrian conservationists studied the origins of the iconic V-shape by focusing on the migration patterns of the northern bald ibis—a critically endangered species of ibis. Fritz showed what scientists had always believed: by observing the ibis over dozens of miles in flight, they were able to show that the birds get two main advantages from the V-formation. First, it allows for each bird to have a clear line of sight to see what's ahead. By maintaining the offset position to the left or right of its nearest forward neighbor, each bird's vision is not obstructed during the flight. The second and maybe most important reason for the shape is that it makes flying over long distances more efficient. Yes, the iconic formation actually helps the birds travel through the air more easily. Scientists discovered that each bird creates a mini-vortex with each flap of its wings. This vortex creates an uplift in the air off to the side of each bird called an upwash.

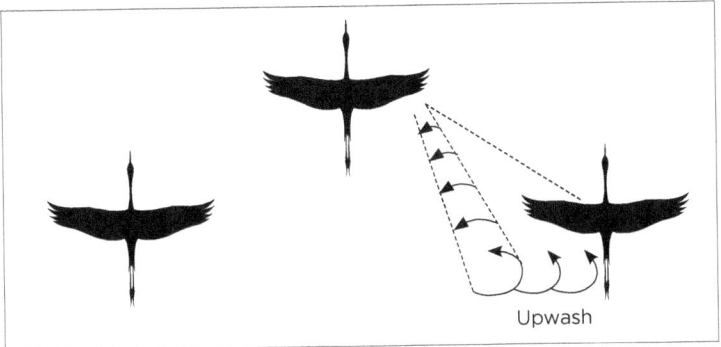

Fig. 2 Create Currents birds upwash.

The birds instinctively position themselves in this sweet spot to get the maximum benefit from the upwash. By being approximately one meter back and one meter to the outside of the bird in front, each bird sits perfectly within the current created by the other. Sitting in the current of others has long been a winning technique in sports, such as NASCAR racing and velodrome cycling, where we call it drafting. Whether it's the V-shape of majestic fowl or cars howling around the oval racetrack of the Indianapolis Motor Speedway, this imagery of positive benefit from others provides a great mental cue for understanding the progression and benefits of currents in our life. It helps to reveal more about this notion of Tool #4. It reminds us how natural currents are and how we can benefit from and help Create Currents for those around us.

Those who know anything about NASCAR racing or team cycling might already be aware that the drafting behind the leader primarily benefits those in the rear of the drafting formation. The same is true for the leader of the flock of birds. For the leading bird in the V-formation, the benefits of the aerodynamic formation do not apply. Studies show that the leading bird in a classic V-shape is often working up to 20 percent harder than the other birds. In order to compensate for this, the birds switch leaders. Birds actually change lead many times over the course of their migratory travels. And this exchange of lead is not specific to that bird's age, experience, or any perceived hierarchy. In fact, the youngest birds in the group also take the lead from time to time, almost like an apprenticeship for someday leading the flock. Who knew birds were so considerate and played fair?

When you think about it, these ibises are not much different than us—aside from their feathers and beaks. Often, we simply need a new leader to emerge to continue propelling us forward. Yes, even for those who are leading today, we must always consider this truth. Leaders change. Situations change. Therefore, modern leaders understand that we can both lead and follow in equal measure.

Remember the Leader's Triangle concept where we talked about leading in our career, family, and community? We rarely have the capacity to lead in all areas of our world equally. We may be active leaders in our family but take a different position in our community or career. Or it may be different for you. You may be a leader amongst your peers at the office but enjoy volunteering for church or other community activities as a follower. In any circumstance, you may experience a situation where you are no longer at the helm as a leader. But the next time you are faced with taking a back seat, think of the V-shape that is so divinely effective. When another leader steps forward, put your pride aside and consider the upwash benefits. Consider the fact that a perceived rival could be just the spark needed to propel you forward.

Just as the ibis who leads in flight has to work harder, being a leader carries its own weight. Let's face it. Leading can be downright tough at times. But as we mature as leaders and continue to understand the forces around us, we also understand that we will not lead in every instance. We often trade our leading positions throughout our lives, and at times, even throughout our day. Once we know this principle well, we also start to relieve ourselves of the internal burden, pressure, and anxiety that can often be associated with taking the lead or leadership. We start to acknowledge that it is equally essential to understand when it is best for others to take the reins. At times, it's in a temporary capacity in an attempt to stretch someone's capability or mold them into future leaders. In other instances, it is the acknowledgment of when being a follower and supporting the current leader is best for everyone. This recognition of change, recognition of role reversal, and recognition that your time will come is also a form of leading. This awareness is often called "leading from the rear." There are times when we need to be comfortable on the wings, following in the current of the ones before us. This is also a noble pursuit, as long as you understand that you can and will lead when the time is right.

WHY DO CURRENTS MATTER?

Whether it's the trade winds that cut through the atmosphere, a current that cuts through the ocean, or social change created by one woman who dared to speak up and say #me-too about sexual assault, all of these currents have two similar characteristics. First, all currents represent some semblance of change. By definition, a current flows differently from its surroundings. A current represents a change in forces or cutting through whatever surrounds it. Simply by trying something new, having a different opinion, taking a different stance, or taking a chance, you can be part of a current that creates tides of change.

Second, currents have a connectedness that helps to provide volume to the current. In nature, many droplets join together to create a current of water that cuts through the river. Without joining together, there is no stream. Without wind gusts being joined in direction, pace, and path, there is no jet stream current high above the Earth's atmosphere. The same applies to social currents and local currents created by humans. It is through our connection to others that we Create Currents in our world. Through the connection of athletic intent and ambition, Bannister, Landy, then all of the middle-distance runners after them were united by a new goal and shared reality. Through a similar connection of ambition, goals, and heritage, Ramachandran and the dozens of Indian-Americans continued the spelling-bee current started by Balu Natarajan.

But why do currents matter to leaders? How do currents help us? How do currents help those around us? Quite simply, currents help accelerate change. The current not only has a momentum that clears the path for others, but it also creates an opportunity for exponential growth in others. Think about it. Once a current is created, no one else needs to start from zero. For those clever enough to carefully follow and position themselves, the upwash is available and provides a less-resistant path forward.

It is this notion of clearing the path for others that is crucial for us as leaders.

LINE-OF-SIGHT CURRENTS

Our personal connection to others is an important aspect of being a leader. In our everyday life, we often use those connections to value and validate our next steps. It is through these personal connections that line-of-sight currents are formed. Like me, having a colleague who wrote a book led me to think differently about the possibility of writing this book; having a direct line of sight with others is a powerful form of *current*.

The term "line of sight" is commonly used in broadcasting to refer to the ability to have an unobstructed visual line from one radio tower to the next. This direct sight allows the radio signal to be received between the chain of buildings, loud and clear. In the same way, this direct connection and proximity of signal can impact the currents we create. In short, the more closely you are associated with a current, the more impact it has on you. What am I trying to say? Quite simply, having a direct, personal connection with someone increases the likelihood of Creating Currents.

It is through our family, our friends, our relationships, our work colleagues, and even our loose association with others that we will create the most powerful and lasting currents. We know the line-of-sight connection and personal rivalry between Roger Bannister and John Landy led to the record-breaking 4-minute mile. It was also through a line-of-sight that I was inspired to spill my thoughts onto a page. But we shouldn't expect for currents to be experienced only through big events or momentous occasions. Yes, that can happen, but it's not the most common way currents work. Yes, it's easier to see the results at the mouth of a river, in the jet stream, and during a hurricane, but the beginning is all the same no matter how big the results. Currents start small.

Currents are not only seen in the extraordinary; they are also created from the day-to-day happenings in life. My mother went from picking cotton in the dusty fields of North Texas as a young girl to being a housekeeper and maid for some of the well-to-do folks in our small town. Then, vowing to give her kids a better life, she worked her way to becoming a data entry clerk at an insurance company, where she worked for over twenty-five years. My mother couldn't have known what currents she was creating in her kids and peers by simply going to work every day.

In this case, "every day" is not figuratively spoken. I mean *every single day*. She was honored by the company for twenty-five years of service without missing a single day of work, except for holidays and having kids. If her dedication isn't enough evidence of her tenacity and consistency that she worked over six thousand consecutive days without calling in sick, she also did this while commuting between one and two hours each day, leaving at 6:00 a.m. and returning home around 6:00 p.m. Incredibly, in her years as a data entry clerk, my mother never changed roles. She never wanted to be a manager or supervisor, although she was offered promotions regularly to recognize her skills and tenure. She was always comfortable in her own skin, choosing to lead herself versus managing others. It is that simple view of diligence and steadfast determination that has inspired me and many others. But that's where currents originate. The smallest rills become channels; then channels become streams; then streams become mighty rivers. What currents are you creating for those around you?

We Create Currents by what we do, how we do it, and through what we say. By committing to do something that is different, we Create Currents. By doing something that we believe in, large or small, we Create Currents. So as a friend, as a colleague, as a manager, as a mother, as a father, as a son, as a daughter . . . know that you already have within you the tools to create an impact. What you do and how you do it matters.

This power to influence and expand the belief of others through what we do is one of our most underrated, underrecognized tools. So go! Chase after the things you love. Take a stand. Enter that contest. Run as fast as you can. Work hard every day, believing that it does, indeed, matter. Go and Create Currents that fill your soul with pride. Create paths you want others to follow. To Create Currents means sparking waves of change. Get out there and use your superpowers for good.

IN RETROSPECT

Tool #4—Create Currents

- This tool is about creating a pathway for others by our actions and ideas—by what we do.
- We looked at currents in the spelling bee, middle-distance running, and migrating birds and how impactful the small details can be.
- We learned that currents impact our beliefs.
- We recognized the benefits of following others. Modern leaders understand that they will both lead and follow.

Practice Leading by Creating Currents

1. Is it time to start creating your path? Do you have an ambition or side hustle that you have set aside? Take the first steps toward tackling that challenging aspect of your career. Do it for yourself, and you will end up inspiring others.

2. Do you lead in every aspect of your life? Or do you tend to follow others even when you know the path? For the next three days, keep a mini-journal of how you lead and follow. Do you need to make a change?

3. Make your voice heard as part of your community. Take a stand for the issues that mean the most to you.

ATTITUDE IS A
LITTLE THING
THAT MAKES A BIG
DIFFERENCE.

—WINSTON CHURCHILL

TOOL #5

Play (PLAy)

As we start to look at Tool #5, it's worth reflecting on what we've accomplished to this point. We are now at the halfway mark in the list of tools for leading yourself and leading others. You are also embarking on one of my favorite tools in this book because we need to loosen up as leaders and relax a bit! As I mentioned before, there is no hard-and-fast rule for the sequence of these tools. However, I did organize the tools, like you might organize tools in your home garage or your toolbox. In a garage, you may consider organizing your household tools by size or type, like putting all of the garden tools together and then all of the power tools together. My garage has never been quite that organized, but I can imagine this is what some people do.

Although these tools and habits have been learned and honed over time, when I sat down to put the ideas into prose, I loosely organized 10LT into two parts. Tools #1–5 are in the section that I call "defining tools." Tools #6–10 are labeled as "refining tools." The defining tools are those tools that help leaders discover more about themselves and promote growth in a leader's journey. They are well-suited to help leaders hungry to learn, develop, and continue to grow in skill and confidence. In comparison, the refining tools are better suited to molding and shaping a person into a more accomplished leader. However, all of the tools in the book do have elements of both defining and refining, so don't get hung up on my grouping.

The significance of Tool #5 is more than the midway point. This tool had to reside in the defining section of the list because it's a fundamental part of our lives as humans, as well as any modern leader's journey. This is also one of those tools that even the most accomplished leader often forgets. Selfishly, I included the tool Play in the first five tools with the hope of highlighting its importance for leaders with varying levels of experience.

The placement of Tool #5 was also about considering life's realities. I know all too well that reading and learning are a commitment. I also know that everyone is incredibly busy with life and constant pressures and challenges, so finishing an entire book for many people is an equal challenge. I thought that by including Tool #5 in the first half of the book, more leaders would get to consume this information before life "happens." Therefore, more leaders will have the power of Play at the ready in their toolbelt.

While I'm confessing about the book's organization, there is another admission I need to make about the tools. Some of you might have noticed that the tools are about action: Tool #1: Use Purpose Over Task; Tool #2: Learn a New Language; Tool #3: Tell Different Stories; Tool #4: Create Currents. Now you can see that Tool #5: Play is no different. These tools are meant to be active because that's what being a leader is all about. It requires active listening, active learning, active connection, and being active in one's career, family, and community. The only thing that separates this one from some of the others that we've covered in prior chapters is that Tool #5 is not only about what we do or how we do it. Tool #5: Play is distinctly centered on making us feel something as well. As we'll learn further in this chapter, the connections formed around Play are unique. It was Maya Angelou who famously said during an interview, "I've learned that people will forget what you said, people will forget what you did, but people will never forget how you made them feel." That is why Play needs to be part of our leader's toolbelt.

Yes, making it to Tool #5 of 10 is a big deal, so congratulate yourself on a job well done. If this were an equivalent moment with my twelve-year-old son, I'd probably give him a nice fist-bump right now. Actually, this moment is more significant than that. It's worth more than a regular fist-bump. We would likely do one of the funky fist-bumps that have the hand-spreading, air explosion, and the accompanying explosive sound effect as our fists separate. That's the level of celebration that you deserve for reaching this tool. Partly because one side of this tool is about just that, taking the time to stop and smell the roses. Yes, reaching this point in this book, or reaching the midway point of any book, is a great excuse to let loose.

Go on, have some playtime. No, I mean it. This is the time to think differently about your life and what it means to be a leader. And the good news is that you now have express consent to play. Yes, young or old, big or small, take the time now to yell, scream, or jump up and down in celebration. I know it's a bit odd, especially if you are reading or listening to this on a crowded bus, but do it anyway. Do something crazy, and just have fun. Likewise, if you are in bed, get up and start jumping and dancing on the bed in celebration. If you are in your living area, turn on some tunes and dance around. Wherever you are in life, wherever you are in this moment, this is your official permission slip to step out and have a bit of fun. Be goofy, be cute, and be quirky. Just do something to enjoy the moment. Don't worry; we'll dive deep into Tool #5: Play when you get back.

CHILD'S PLAY

I hope that moment of wild and crazy fun was good for you. If not, let's look at why crazy in the form of Play is cool (or *CrazySexyCool*, for those TLC fans out there). Think back to your childhood. What memories come to mind? Now recall your childhood and specifically think about the moments that made you happy. Think about the moments of enjoyment or freedom. Think about the moments of fun. Which moments come flooding to the surface for you? In most cases, these moments of joy, craziness, happiness, and frivolity involved elements of play. When I think about these moments for myself, many thoughts seep to the surface through the whitewash of memories that I have as a boy.

One of the few glimpses of true memories includes me playing with a record player. Yes, a genuine record player. I see myself playing with a seven-inch vinyl. I also remember needing to place a penny or a dime on top of the record player's needle head to keep the needle in place to prevent the songs from skipping.

This memory stands out because my mother once showed me an old Polaroid picture of me playing with that small turntable. In my head, I still see myself with headphones over my small, well-shaped afro. I was under ten years old, sitting there, loving life, and looking at the camera with a sheepish smile. I remember how much fun I had listening to music on that player. It was a special feeling.

Another personal memory is playing "chase" or, as some would call it, "tip" with my friends down Emma Jane Street in my childhood neighborhood. It was a quiet street, so playing on the road was a standard extension to any sporting activity. I also have flashes of memories of running in front of my brother while we played, and the only objective of the game was for the chaser to touch the other person . . . the chased. Once anyone has been touched by the chaser, that person becomes the chaser, and the cycle continues until everyone is exhausted. It's a simple game, but it's so much fun. However, this memory stands out because, for some unknown reason, this time, we decided to play with the chaser riding a bicycle while the others ran on foot. I'm not sure if that's fair, but it seemed logical at the time, especially to us kids.

In this memory, I recall the day when my brother Rick chased me down the street as I ran right in front of his bike, and he pursued me with a big smile on his face. I was little but quick and agile, weaving left and right to avoid being caught by my big brother. I was running and laughing, and then everything stopped with a bang. I tripped while my brother was only inches behind me. Landing face-first on the black gravel road, I could feel the nubbly tread of Rick's BMX bicycle wheels as they rolled over my backside.

I don't remember much after that point. I don't remember any of the pain. I have no memory of crying or picking out pebbles of gravel from my bloody wounds that extended from my bare feet to my face. I don't remember what excuse we gave our mother for why our version of bike versus boy had superseded traditional chase. I don't remember if Rick got grounded for running his little brother over with a bike, but I do have lasting memories of the moment. My memories go beyond the physical scars that I still have on my knees and elbows today. I have the memory of how daring, fun, and free we were in the streets of the "Rocks," as we called Rockwall, Texas. When the feeling of connection to my childhood, hometown, friends, and family comes flooding back, it reminds me of the power of Play.

WHAT IS PLAY?

The concept of Play is very familiar when we look at the lives of children. When you think of what it means to watch children play, we have a universal understanding of that and what it could mean. Do you picture kids running or chasing each other? Or maybe it's a toddler sitting on the floor and playing with toys? Whatever image comes to mind, we would all generally agree with that image of playing. But when I say the word "play" for adults, what comes to mind? A consistent understanding of play amongst adults is far more elusive. This is what Dr. Stuart Brown from the National Institute for Play explored in his research that reviewed over six thousand participants. Brown studied the role that play has in a person's childhood and adulthood which he calls "play histories." What Brown discovered is that play, or the lack of play, can profoundly impact who we are.

First, let us explore what we mean by the word "play" since it can conjure different meanings for different people. Brown describes play in his book, *Play: How It Shapes the Brain, Opens the Imagination, and Invigorates the Soul*. Instead of a specific definition, Brown offers some properties of play as a starting point: "Here are the properties of play. Apparent purposelessness, done for its own sake, voluntary, inherent, attraction, freedom from time, diminished consciousness of self, improvisational potential, continuation desire." In the book, he continues to explain that the concept of play is unique because all or some of these properties exist in some form to constitute what we know as play.

"It's all around us yet goes mostly unnoticed or unappreciated until it is missing," Brown further explains, and this is why play is an essential tool for leading. Play is one of the most overlooked tools in the arsenal of leaders, so it's important to understand the benefits of Play, especially as adults. Because Play isn't just an action; it isn't just doing for the sake of doing, especially if we benefit from it. All of the things that we may recognize as playing for adults, like fun and frivolity, banter, laughter, and jokes, create a distinct chemical reaction in the brain that makes it different from other activities throughout your day. Just like telling an attention-grabbing story, as we discussed in Tool #3, the laughter associated with Play can release the chemicals in our brain that create lasting empathic connections like oxytocin, dopamine, and endorphins. Play can help us feel more connected to a person, a team, or a situation. This is what makes Play so important to us as a tool for leaders. We may not realize it, but we need the power of Play.

Try another exercise with me. Ask yourself: "When was the last time I played as an adult?" Excluding fun and frivolity with children involved, when was the last time you did something that allowed you to have a deep belly laugh? If you can think of something from less than twenty-four hours ago, then congratulations. If you thought of your craziness from the beginning of this chapter, even better. If it was harder for you, then it's time to be purposeful about interjecting more playful fun into your day and into your week. Do it for your family or within the context of your career or your business, but whatever you do, choose more Play.

MAKE IT FUN

The music was so loud that it vibrated my chest with every rhythmic beat. As I made my way toward the source of the heart-pounding music, there stood an imposing gray shipping container that took center stage in the empty field. Hordes of people had gathered, transfixed as they watched magnetically charged bearded bakers make magic with ingredients. The makeshift bakery was clad with murals painted on the outside walls of the shipping container. Custom-made steel doors were flung open to reveal the magic inside. As I drew closer, I saw the crowd queued up to be served on one side of the bakery counter while others gathered in a semicircle watching the spectacle. Some were dancing; others were clapping and stomping to the rhythm of the infectious combination of Middle Eastern, pop, and R&B tunes emanating from the onsite DJ. The few people that weren't on their feet were grooving while camped out on picnic blankets, beach chairs, and old milk crates like a summer concert on the lawn. The crowd was fixated like adoring fans at a music festival, swept up in the moment as they watched the guys known as the Bearded Bakers make desserts.

My wife is a pastry chef and baker by trade, so we have spent a lifetime sampling and searching out delicious treats, cakes, and pastries in the name of "research." It's the type of research that is not great for the waistline, but admittedly there are far worse vices to have. Whenever traveling or on vacation, we make a point of always sampling the local bakeries. Our research has taken us to hundreds of bakeries in our years of marriage, including patisseries and bread shops around the world, from Sarlat-la-Canéda in the Dordogne region of France to the renowned cafés of Amsterdam, to small, inspiring patisseries in Connecticut. But this bakery in the heart of Sydney was like none we had ever seen.

Stepping up to this bakery felt like being a part of an entertainment event, and the atmosphere was electric. Everywhere around us, we saw a sea of smiling faces, laughter, dancing, and yes, eating the one and only dish served at this unique bakery: a creamy, sweet, cheesy dessert called knafeh. Donning crisp white aprons and long hipster beards, the bakers danced, laughed, and interacted with their customers in a way that I've never seen. We were in awe.

As the team of bearded men moved and gyrated with the beat of the music, they were artfully assembling hundreds of the warm crème-brûlèe-like desserts topped with crumbled pistachios and fragrant sugar syrup for their adoring crowd. The

Knafeh Bakery, run by Ameer El-issa, his brother, Joey, and his sister, Mouna, is a bakery with Play at the center of their success. This traveling theatre-come-bakery is a unique enterprise that demonstrates the power of using fun and frivolity to create connective teamwork and an unmatched customer experience. This bakery is not just famous for its food. It's a place that is even more famous for creating memories and bringing smiles to the faces of its customers and everyone involved. The Knafeh Bakery team understands the value of Play.

You may be thinking to yourself, *How does this relate to me? I could never see myself dancing and having fun at my job or in my office.* But that's exactly why this tool is so important. We need to reconnect with Play as part of our life at work, on the field, or at home. So many of us don't know the value of Play or have simply forgotten how good it feels. But this tool is about reminding us to think differently. In all of our efforts to live, pay bills, resolve issues, get that report done, and be responsible, we have somehow lost the ability to play, relax, tell a joke, and have a laugh. In some instances, it's because we see playing as juvenile or irresponsible; in other cases, it's just not something we think about. No matter your reason for losing your sense of Play, it's something you need to get back in your life, especially as a leader. To Play as an adult is not easy. It is not as natural as it is for children, so we must work at it.

This is where the other side of Tool #5 (PLAy) comes in: Purpose-Led Attitude. As an adult and as a leader, PLAy is only made possible through a series of choices, and when those choices align with your purpose, it can create magic. Play within the adult realm is not only something we can do to make our world better; it's a choice we need to make regularly. Having a Purpose-Led Attitude allows you to go to work on those grumpy days. Having a Purpose-Led Attitude allows you to see a setback as temporary. It allows your attitude to be ultimately driven by where you are going versus what you can see right now. Using PLAy allows you to look beyond your situation and use purpose as the North Star for your attitude. What is "attitude?" It is your internal or outward expression of emotion. Attitude is the posture, mindset, or feelings you apply to a given situation. You can have a positive attitude or a negative attitude. It's your choice. I don't know the team at the Knafeh Bakery personally, but I can bet you that they have as many problems as you and I. They probably have dramas with their kids, with their relationships, with their peers, and everything in between. But the team at Knafeh has learned how to come to work with the right attitude. They know what's important. They know that no matter how crappy the day has been, they have chosen to deliver an incredible experience to their customers. They have chosen a Purpose-Led Attitude.

We have all heard the phrase "fake it till you make it," right? The phrase may be trite, but the principle is sound. PLAy enables us to change the internal dialogue to match our outward expression. Using the tool, Purpose-Led Attitude simply reminds us that we have a choice. We can choose how we behave. We can choose how we react. We can choose how we interact with others. PLAy allows us to connect our outward attitude to our internal purpose. This becomes even more important as we work with others. As a leader, the fun can not only have a purpose but be driven by that purpose. Having a reason that affords us those moments of levity, those times of pure pleasure, laughter, and passion are all enhanced by aligning those moments to purpose.

WHAT IS PURPOSE?

I know we've talked about purpose in a couple of tools now, so I'd better give you my take on what that means. It was mentioned in Tool #1: Purpose Over Task, and now again as part of Tool #5: Play. In the context of 10LT, what exactly is meant by "purpose?" I'll be honest, the meaning of purpose is probably as elusive and varied as the true understanding of leadership. The topic of purpose or how to find purpose has also had countless articles and books to describe what it is or how you find yours. However, I have a view on purpose that is simple and unrefined, but it works for me. And it is how you should view your purpose in this book.

First, know that purpose is not the same for everyone, so knowing one's purpose is a very personal thing. Second, purpose can evolve over time. I believe that our purpose will change as our life situation changes. To me, purpose is the intersection between who you are and the impact you want to have on the world around you. I'll say it again to make sure you fully grasp the statement. One's purpose is the intersection between who you are and the impact you want to have on the world around you. So what does that mean? Like many of you, I once believed that my purpose would be revealed like a revelation from God or from a James Earl Jones type of voice booming from the clouds or in my head. I also once believed that my purpose would be absolute, and once I discovered it, that was it. I believed I would follow that one true purpose, forever. But I no longer believe that. I now believe that, yes, some very lucky people know and find their purpose early in life. I've heard of people who knew from an early age that they wanted to be a doctor, for example. But is that purpose or a career? I guess if you know the underlying reason for becoming a doctor is to help people, then you can definitely say it's a purpose. Either way, some people do discover purpose through divine intervention, but many of us do not. That is why I started to rethink what purpose meant.

Upon reflecting on how we travel through life and experience purpose, this view of purpose being an intersection as part of our life journey became clearer. To help visualize this concept, imagine your life as a long, winding road. Then imagine you're taking a trip down that road, and you encounter many intersections. These intersections represent various life events. Some are good, and some are not. The intersections could represent people who impact your life, personal discoveries, times of joy and revelation, or times of pain and sadness. Some are impactful, and others are just providing experience, knowledge, and the overall structure of your life. This winding road of events and encounters is how I view purpose in our lives. I believe our purpose is revealed when we cross paths with something or someone that changes us. When one of life's intersections changes how we think, then that purpose is revealed. Your purpose is shaped and designed by the events of your life, including what you have suffered or equally how you've been saved. Yes, it is possible to find purpose while we seek clarity, but often purpose finds us. I also believe that purpose can change as we encounter other situations and circumstances that shape our lives. It's based on your experiences, what you've witnessed, your challenges, the good and bad of your life. For some people, including myself, our purpose will have seasons and will change as life situations change. One's purpose is an expansion of your sense of identity.

On reflection, I think back on my "supposed" grand purpose as a young adult and how vastly different it is from my purpose now as a community contributor, leader, entrepreneur, husband, and father. I also believe my career purpose can be different from what it is in my community life or my family life. So as I talk about purpose in the pages of this book, know that I'm not talking about the elusive, mystical, magical unknown. I'm talking about your purpose today. Remember Jenny, the custodian at Disneyland, who wanted to make a little girl happy? Remember Wiley Post, who wanted a better life and loved airplanes? Like them, our purpose is found as we discover the world we want to change, in big or small ways. I'm talking about the impact you want to have in your world. That's your purpose. And it's within you, based on who you are today (and the intersections in your journey) as well as where you want to go.

But like any journey, the road ahead helps us imagine where we are headed or who we want to be—or maybe even who we could be. You have a purpose now. You have a purpose, no matter what you have been told. You have a purpose, no matter what you have told yourself. Use Tool #5 freely. Use the power of Play to your advantage in your daily life, in your book club, at your restaurant, with your partner. Create moments of fun and laughter, knowing that at that moment, you are being purpose-led. Then let your attitude and actions pave the way to lasting memories and deeper connections. Go and live that purpose, but do it with style by sprinkling in dashes of Play, fun, and pure joy along the way.

IN RETROSPECT

Tool #5—Play and PLAy

- This tool calls us to remember that fun and joy should be a part of our daily journey as a leader. It also encourages us to adopt an attitude guided by purpose.
- Play can release beneficial chemicals in our brain, like oxytocin, dopamine, and endorphins.
- We learned about a bakery with Play at the center of its business.
- PLAy represents the importance of a Purpose-Led Attitude.
- We learned about purpose and how to align our daily attitude with that purpose.

Practice Leading with Play (PLAy)

1. In the office, start your recurring team meeting with a joke of the day or week.
2. For a full seven days, ask your spouse or anyone in the family, "What made you laugh today?" Then have them do the same for you. If there are not enough open-mouthed belly laughs, insert more Play immediately.
3. Music is a great way to experience Play. Try playing a song of the day at your office to get people out of their seats for a daily stretch and dance. I once worked in a team that blasted a song at ten o'clock each weekday morning, and we all took turns selecting the tunes.

> THERE IS VIRTUE IN WORK, AND THERE IS VIRTUE IN REST. USE BOTH AND OVERLOOK NEITHER.

—ALAN COHEN

TOOL #6

Pulse

Your heart beats over 100,000 times per day. It relentlessly performs the rhythm of life by pumping blood throughout our bodies. It expands and contracts to pump up to six quarts of blood per minute. That's two thousand gallons per day! Our hearts will beat over 2.5 billion times in our lifetime, and in most of us, this happens without us noticing. But once this perfect pattern of precision is broken, we sit up and take notice. When our heart skips a beat, we notice. When our heart races, we take notice. And if that constant pumping stops, the results can be devastating. Yes, we certainly take notice then. But 99.99 percent of the time, our bodies are divinely created to perform this work for us. The body is a miraculous machine.

Aside from something unusual or dramatic happening, our beating heart is constant and predictable. Whenever we want to measure how our heart is performing, good or bad, we gauge our heart rate by taking our pulse. From deep within our chest, our heart pushes blood through our bodies, and a rhythm is established. That rhythm is what we can feel through the physical sensation on the surface of the skin that we call a pulse. This concept of measuring the pulse was first documented in ancient Greece by physicians and scientists. The first person credited with measuring or timing the pulse was Herophilus of Alexandria, Egypt (c. 335 BC–280 BC), who designed an ancient water clock that was purpose-built to help time the rhythm and frequency of the pulse.

The pulse can be measured in many areas of the body, such as the neck. One of the most common places is on the wrist. Some of you would have tried this before, but let's do this together. To measure your pulse, place two fingers on the inside of your opposite wrist just below the thumb. As your fingers rest against your wrist, focus and feel the tiny thumps of the artery pushing and contracting. That is your pulse. If you want to know your pulse rate, have a phone or another timer nearby and count how many thumps you feel in thirty seconds, then multiply that number by two. Or just look at your fitness watch!

Along with the wrist, a pulse can be measured at the groin, behind the knee, or near the ankle joint of the foot. These are all areas where we can physically feel the thumping sensation of a pulse. This thump is the result of a beating heart as it pushes blood through the arteries, and those arteries first expand and then contract with the flow of blood. By taking our pulse, what we feel is not only the physical expansion and contraction of blood. By taking our pulse, we measure the rhythm of our lives.

The word "pulse" is not only used to describe the rhythmic expansion of our arteries as our blood is pushed through the body. Even sound vibrations, light waves, electrical currents, or anything that has a rhythmic drive can be said to have a pulse.

And it is through this rhythm or repetition, through this cycle of push and rest, that we start to understand how mastery of Tool #6 can be of benefit to anyone, especially leaders.

Think about the entire process involved in what we describe as a pulse. It's about the heart's ability to push and then rest. Push and rest. For those of you who tried it at the beginning of this chapter, we experienced this rhythm firsthand by placing the fingers from one hand against your other wrist. And for those of us who are not trained in CPR or part of the medical profession, it may have been your first time feeling this rhythm since, ordinarily, it happens without us knowing. Even if you didn't feel your pulse, you know it's happening. God has created this magical mechanism that works for us day and night, and it's occurring over thirty-five million times a year. This tells us that as human beings, we are tuned for this cadence of push and rest. Push and rest. Let's explore this further as we get to the heart of the matter with Tool #6. (See what I did there?)

Now that you know more about the heart's incredible ability to pump life-giving blood throughout the body, what is the relationship with 10LT? Many of you are thinking, *Thanks for reminding me why I hated biology in school. But what is Tool #6, Pulse, all about?* Metaphorically, Tool #6 represents you. Tool #6 represents me. It represents all of us in some way. Think back to what is happening in our arteries each second, then think about your life. In life, we have times of extreme pressure. We have moments of going beyond our limits, moments of stretching ourselves, moments of pushing for something extremely hard. That's the push.

Now think about the other part of the pulse rhythm: the rest. In life, there is always a need for rest. No, not only by sleeping at night or the kind of rest that occurs when you take a vacation each year. We need rest as part of our day-to-day rhythm. We need rest alongside the push. Our bodies demand it. Our minds demand it. Yes, the Pulse should be the rhythm of life, both inside and out, and most of us don't understand how to use its cadence to our advantage.

What does that mean for us as people? What does that mean for us as modern leaders? It means that we should expect the push that comes as a normal part of life. We should expect that stress will come. Times of pressure and pain will be part of life, but we must insert some space or rest in our world in order to be successful. It's this rest, this downtime, these periods of meditation and reflection that help make those tough times manageable. Now, I want to be clear. This is not my attempt to say that we need a work-life balance. Frankly, I don't believe in that whole work-life balance thing since modern life is rarely balanced.

However, I certainly believe in taking every step possible to manage all aspects of one's life. My view is that we must be intentional in our efforts to keep our family life, our community contributions, and our career or personal aspirations in sync. And that synchronization doesn't necessarily equate to a perfect balance. There simply will be times when one area of your life completely dominates the others. But although it is not ideal, I see it as part of modern life and the human condition.

In my experience, to get the best that life has to offer while also getting the best from us as people, we need the same things that our bodies are designed for. We need to push and be pushed on certain occasions to help strengthen our mental and emotional muscles. That means there are sure to be times when we need to work extremely hard. We'll be forced to work harder than we want to, harder than we think we should have to, but we must do it to achieve growth. At the risk of sounding too clichéd, we need to "put in the work for anything that is worth having." And it is rarely balanced by any measure. But the best leaders and the most successful people have figured out ways to handle life's stresses. They've demonstrated how to avoid being overwhelmed and how to quieten the noise. The best leaders have designed their lives to have some rest to complement the push. In fact, adding a Pulse routine has been proven to have a number of both physical and mental benefits. Studies show that including routine meditation can reduce mental stress and anxiety. Still, other studies attribute Pulse patterns like prayer and mindful reflection to physical benefits, such as pain reduction and reduced blood pressure in patients.

Without providing respite to our constant mental and physical stimuli, I believe our personal growth can be stunted. Think about the human body and how nature dictates a particularly strong Pulse regime. Aside from our heartbeat, every breath follows the same pattern as our lungs expand and rest. The average adult is awake for sixteen to eighteen hours a day, but we must sleep at some point. This rest gained through sleep helps our bodies and minds reset and repair, but it is not a choice; it is a part of our biological makeup. We can think of these bodily Pulse rhythms as the blueprint for humans. Even our muscles are perfected by using the Pulse principle. During strength training or any strenuous exercise, muscle tissue is stretched and torn. However, muscles only grow stronger and bigger during the muscle repair process or rest. Just like in life, we are growing, stretching ourselves, pushing ourselves to the limit, but there is no true growth without the ability to stop, rest, and reflect.

I always like to look at nature in pursuit of understanding more about how we work as humans. Consider the cheetah. It is one of the big cats native to Africa and Iran, but most wild cheetahs can be found in sub-Saharan Africa. The cheetah is widely known as one of the fastest animals on the face of the Earth, reaching speeds of up to seventy miles per hour, and it can do this in under three seconds. But even the mighty cheetah uses the Pulse principle to refine its pursuits.

Adult cheetahs can be over 1.5 yards in length and weigh well over one hundred pounds. The feline's pale-yellow coat and black dots help it blend perfectly into dry, arid lands as well as slip into the shadows as they roam grassy Saharan plains or forests. But it's not the cheetah's camouflage that makes them fierce predators; it's their speed. This is an animal designed for speed. Evolution has allowed the cheetah to develop long muscular legs and a slender body with a uniquely flexible spine that allows the body of the cheetah to extend and twist at extreme angles while at top running speeds.

Once the cheetah spots pray with its keen eyesight, it can use its slender, wiry build and long legs to accelerate to top speeds. It also uses its long, muscular tail, measuring up to thirty-five inches, like a counterbalance to help it navigate offensive maneuvers with a certain grace and agility. Like the cheetah, many of us are born to run. Maybe not physically run, but through our ambition, through our determination, through our workaholic tendencies.

But even the mighty cheetah has to surrender to the Pulse paradigm. The cheetah reaches top speeds in an attempt to catch its prey, but it can only sustain that pace for a short period. Just like us, the cheetah uses a lot of focus and energy during its pursuits. And nature has a way of regulating that energy, so the cheetah can only sprint at its peak for less than a minute, usually for a distance of three hundred yards. And if the cheetah has not achieved its goal of capturing its prey, it mindfully stops its pursuit to rest and run again another day.

Our goal as leaders is to ensure we are performing at our peak, just like the cheetah. Tool #6 is about helping us fine-tune every part of our lives by practicing Pulse. Tool #6 is about finding ways to build this Pulse pattern into your daily life. How do you make Pulse a pattern? Often, the first thing that I hear in response to this question is, "I make sure I take a nice, long vacation once a year." Yes, this is a perfect opportunity to rest. But the key to Pulse in the context of this book is to build it into your normal existence, into your normal daily rhythm, as a pattern or habit that you can rely on. Unfortunately, although important, taking days off work for a holiday still leaves us without rest in our day-to-day lives. To Pulse as a tool is much more than simply taking time off. Pulse is about being able to industrialize the process of pushing, resting, renewal, and reflection. Repeat.

There are many ways to build in a routine that allows for rest. Some people pray. Some people simply sit in silence. Others use deep breathing techniques, and others find going for a run, hitting the gym, or doing yoga restful. Still, others find reflection while chanting, saying mantras, or other forms of meditation to create space. You may include any or all of these forms of reflection in your day or in your week, but whatever you do, make sure there is a constant source of pause inserted into your routine. Remember, the goal is not necessarily to balance. Continue to push extremely hard when acting with purpose. Continue to pursue your goals and dreams at full pace, but help sustain that pace by being intentional. Insert your personal Pulse pattern to keep your mind, body, and spirit at their peak.

For those of you having trouble imagining some type of pause or meditation in your daily routine, maybe this simple example will help. Think of our body and mental state like that of a mobile phone. I know it's a bit of a stretch, but work with me for a moment. Consider this: We use our mobile phones in so many ways, and for some of us, it is an essential part of our lives. It doesn't matter whether you use your mobile phone for social media or work or just for keeping in touch with friends and family; we all see the value in keeping our mobile phones charged. Think of how you feel when you really need your mobile phone, but the battery is running low. We've all had that sinking feeling when our phone warns us that we have only 2 percent battery charge remaining, and it always comes at the most inopportune time. Maybe the warning comes in the middle of an important conversation, or maybe while using the map for driving directions. No matter the reason we needed the phone, that 2 percent battery notification is never a pleasing sight. What's interesting is that our mobile devices are pretty smart and would have also given us similar warnings at other intervals—first with 20 percent battery remaining, then with 10 percent. So why did we let the battery get so low? If the mobile device is such an important part of our daily equation, why didn't we keep it charged?

Most of you are thinking, *KG, it's obvious. If there was a power outlet or spare battery around, I would have charged the phone. Duh!* But when there is not a power source around or the right accessories around, there's nothing we can do. In other words, you would not purposely let the mobile phone battery get low, and you would have charged it before it got so low if you had the means. Now think about a similar situation in your life where you needed to be creative or come up with an idea, but those ideas just didn't come. You may have been in an environment where you were under pressure and needed to deliver, and you just fell short.

These are situations that I call "low-battery moments." It is only when these important things occur that we realize how important it is to be fully charged. Any other time, our low-battery warnings from our body or mind don't get the attention they likely deserve. But it's when you need it that having the discipline of Pulse really shines. You must think about your Pulse routine like your mobile phone. Just like the phone, most of us religiously recharge every single night. Why? Because we need to rely on it. So when it comes to our human batteries, our capacity to learn, and our ability to lead, we also need recharging regularly. We need something consistent and predictable. This is how we can think of permitting ourselves to insert the power to Pulse.

For those experienced leaders reading this book, you'll already know how difficult this can be. But my view is that this is hard to master for anyone in the modern world. We are all so busy and so ambitious in our personal or career pursuits that adding in anything else seems impossible, even if we are adding the opportunity for that much-needed space. Tool #6 is not something that is mastered without being deliberate. Just like migrating birds flying in the familiar V-shape, at some point, the leading bird must know when it is time to reduce the strain associated with leading the pack. The lead bird must take a calculated step back to rest on the currents created by others.

As I learned more about the benefits of Pulse, I have discovered a few different ways to do this over the years. There are times that I start my day with a simple prayer for peace and serenity. Other times, I have tried practical and straightforward approaches, like having "downtime" added as a one-hour recurring meeting in my personal or office calendar to start the Pulse process. Another approach that I've perfected over the years is a form of meditation. Although I will admit it is not a traditional meditation, it still allows for respite and reflection.

Like so many of us, I spend hours commuting to and from a client site or my office every week. And during my commute, I usually listen to some type of music, audiobook, or podcast. But in an attempt to practice the art of Pulse, I have a reminder three times per week in the morning and twice weekly during the evening commute to listen to nothing. Yes, nothing. If I'm driving, I turn off the sound and let the road noise and traffic sounds fill the air. When I'm on public transportation, like the bus or train, I mute the sound on my mobile phone while keeping my headphones on. Yes, I keep the headphones on with nothing playing in my ears. I know that sounds too simplistic, but trust me, it's incredibly powerful when you practice unplugging regularly.

This form of modern meditation allows me to be in my regular environment but transcend my thoughts. And whether driving on my own or riding in a crowded bus, I find there is just enough white noise around me to make the meditation effective. It's similar to relaxing your way into sleep by listening to white noise, falling rain, or ocean waves as a base to center and still the mind. I try to be diligent with this and other Pulse routines to free my mind of the day's worries. I try to release the stress with this meditation and rest.

However, the question remains: "If this has such potential to benefit us, why is the practice of Pulse so rare?" The answer is disturbingly simple. I don't know about you, but I was never taught how to rest. I was never taught to sit and meditate. I was only taught to work hard. I was taught that "if you work hard, you can do anything" and "hard work pays off." This has also been echoed by society in the form of classic movies like *Rocky* and *The Karate Kid*. So I understand the reason why we feel we should always push. I understand that to succeed in life, I need to stretch myself to grow, to learn, and to change constantly. I get that. And if you are reading this book, you probably get it too.

But this Pulse concept of rest is different. Yes, the peak of the Pulse likely comes much more naturally than it should. But what about the break, the silence, the rest? I don't have a catchy phrase for that. Where are the posters on the wall touting the benefits of rest? Where are the movies that resonate through generations and extol the benefits of meditation and self-reflection? I can tell you: They don't exist. They don't exist because we are taught that rest is weakness. We are taught that pushing, fighting, and grinding it out are good. And resting, taking a break, and stopping to reset must be the opposite of that, right?

Simply put, any period of rest, renewal, or time spent not doing something is typically regarded as lazy or unengaged. If we take a break, we are somehow not working as hard as our peers. This has been the problem for decades, and this is what causes us to push and push without recognizing the need for rest. We are like the cheetah that uses all its energy to get to top speeds, but as humans, we think we know better than nature. We have overridden any natural mechanism that tells us to stop and rest. We keep pushing and pushing until our body gives out or our minds no longer have the capacity to grow, learn, and accept change. Unfortunately, for those of you who are already successful in your career or have achieved success in life without recharging, your ability to acknowledge the need for a Pulse routine becomes even harder. Success breeds comfort. Success tends to support this self-dialog: "If it ain't broke, don't fix it." Therefore the unhealthy pattern of push with no pause continues. But let me be the first to tell you in the words of author Marshall Goldsmith: "What got you here won't get you there." When we consider the many reasons to embrace Tool #6, another great story comes to mind that may help you understand the "why" behind this tool.

TOO FULL

I was told the story of a great Zen master from long ago. The master was known around the world for his wisdom and teachings. One day, an important newspaper reporter from New York was sent to visit the master. He was commissioned in hopes of writing a feature story about his customs and Zen practices. After a two-day journey, the reporter arrived at the master's temple only to be greeted by one of the master's assistants, who told the reporter that the master would speak to him tomorrow. This annoyed the reporter, who was also quite famous for his books and articles. The next day rolled around, and yet again, the master's assistant told the reporter that the master was unavailable and would not be able to speak to him until the following day. By the third day, the reporter's patience had worn thin, so upon seeing the assistant come to greet him, he demanded to see the master. "I am wasting my time with you when I should be speaking to the master. I am one of the most influential reporters in the world, and he should be begging me to interview him. This is not acceptable. I demand to see him now!" the reporter boomed in his most authoritative voice.

Hearing the reporter raise his voice at the assistant, the master agreed to see the reporter that evening. When evening came, and the reporter entered the master's quarters, the reporter immediately began asking questions about Zen and the ways of Zen. Still, the master simply listened and remained silent. The reporter once again started to show his frustration toward the master and said, "I have traveled thousands of miles and taken the time to come here, and after three days, I have learned nothing from you. Nothing." At that point, the master smiled and nodded, then broke his silence by asking the reporter, "Can I pour you some tea?" The reporter was astonished since these were the first words from the master. "Ah, yes," he replied, thinking this seemed like a great step forward for them. The master meticulously placed two cups on the table in front of them. He then began to pour tea into the cup nearest the reporter. As the master was pouring the tea, the reporter continued in his line of questioning. The master remained silent but poured and poured the tea until it rose to the rim. His pouring continued until the tea spilled over the edge, then onto the table, and finally on the floor near the reporter. The reporter, in disbelief, shouted at the master, "Stop! Enough! Are you blind? Can't you see what you're doing? The cup is full already!" The master then stopped pouring and looked up at the reporter with a nod and slight smile. "Yes, you are like this teacup. You are already full—full of your own opinions, your own thoughts, your own ways, and nothing else can be added. Come back to me when your cup is empty."

What do you think the Zen master wanted to teach the reporter? This story is an excellent reminder that we need to create space in our world: space to learn, space to think, space to absorb, and space to grow. Now ask yourself, "Am I too full?" Is your social media or television habit keeping you filled? Have you spent too much time putting things in your proverbial cup without taking time to empty it by using elements of pause, rest, and reflection? This is a perfect time for you, your family, and your team to consider how to build a lifelong habit of Pulse into your daily life.

IN RETROSPECT

Tool #6—Pulse

- This tool is about using the body's natural rhythms to guide us to both push and rest.
- We learned the mental and physical benefits of regular meditation and mindfulness.
- We learned a few modern meditation tools and techniques.
- We asked, "Is my cup too full?"

Practice Leading with Pulse

1. How much time do you have to be still and reflect each day? Ask yourself this question, and then make a plan to carve out at least thirty minutes per day. If you are a beginner, try to designate time first thing in the morning, which may be easier to maintain.

2. At the job, plan for time to pause and reflect for your team. One approach I've seen work well is to have Pulse time built into the department schedule each week (or fortnightly). Each week you can designate four hours, or half a day, for reflection time, downtime, creative time, or whatever you want to call it.

3. In your community group or sports team, remind everyone to spend time for themselves, then add a moment of silence before each meeting or practice session.

WE ARE WHAT WE
REPEATEDLY DO.
EXCELLENCE, THEN,
IS NOT AN ACT BUT
A HABIT.

—WILL DURANT

TOOL #7

Be Vanilla

As we noticed as part of Tool #6: Pulse, consistency is a critical part of any leader's journey. The benefit of rest and reflection is only fully realized by creating that rhythm of consistency. So it's only appropriate that we start to explore this concept of consistency through Tool #7: Be Vanilla. As I've mentioned before, there is no specific order to the way these tools, rules, and habits should be learned, listed, or used. However, embracing Tool #7 can go a long way toward mastering any other tool. It is that powerful. In some respects, I would consider this tool a subtext to almost any other tool you want to master. In other words, the concept of Being Vanilla should be the foundation for you to build upon. Whether it's learning or leading or just living, I don't believe it is an overstatement to say that through Tool #7, greatness is born.

If you are not a foodie or married to one like I am, you may not be as familiar with what it takes to produce one of the most revered and expensive spices in the world, second only to saffron: vanilla. So let me clue you in. It takes three to five years for the vanilla plant to first begin producing an orchid that only flowers one morning per year. Farmers must be diligent in checking the vine-like crops daily in search of the pale-white flower. Once a flowering orchid is located, the flower must be pollinated by hand through a delicate technique discovered in 1841 and still used today. If the flower is somehow missed during its slim window of bloom lasting only a few hours, the precious flower will simply wilt and die, missing its opportunity to produce vanilla for the year. Only if the farmer's attempt to mimic the natural pollination technique of the wild Mexican bee is successful, the fruit will develop in five to six weeks and mature, ready for harvest in six to nine months. Once harvested, the pods are finally prepared for the intricate process to blanch, sweat, dry, and cure the beans for up to six more weeks before readying the spice for export. Yes, it takes time, patience, and consistency to be in the vanilla game. Likewise, it takes the same time and effort to Become Vanilla as a part of your personal toolbelt.

The year was 2018, and the price of vanilla hit an all-time high. The talk amongst savvy investors was whether silver or vanilla was a wiser investment. It was the eye-watering price tag and the meteoric rise of the lowly vanilla pod to over $600 per kilogram that caused such an unusual debate. I was acutely aware of the fluctuation in the price of vanilla because my wife owned a bakery at the time, which was dramatically impacted by the "bounce of the bean." Yes, there were plenty of inexpensive artificial vanilla flavorings available, but as a chef who takes pride in baking with authentic flavors, this was a problem. Suddenly, customer favorites like vanilla-butter cake and vanilla bean icings were some of the most expensive products to make.

The vanilla bean bull run was not only felt in my household; it was also felt by home bakers, chefs, restaurateurs, and customers across the globe.

The price spike for vanilla was due to a combination of factors. First, simple supply and demand. About 60 to 80 percent of the world's vanilla production is from the remote island of Madagascar. This fact alone makes vanilla unique. But add in major weather events like Cyclone Enawo that hit in 2017 and destroyed many of the prized crops, and it became even harder to meet the world's demands. The other reason for the incredible spike was the "degree of difficulty score" that vanilla gets amongst the spice world. Vanilla is extremely hard to produce. It takes a very specific process in a very specific climate. So it was this perfect storm of factors that made vanilla the darling of the spice trade at the time. But it was not always this way.

Vanilla, despite its delightful flavor and reverence amongst the culinary community, has a checkered past. The word "vanilla" has become synonymous with plain, basic, or unexciting. But how is this possible? How is a precious spice known specifically for its flavor-enhancing properties since the early seventeenth century now known for being just the opposite?

In the dictionary, you'll find it used as an adjective describing the simplest version of something, basic or ordinary. The fate of the vanilla label didn't happen all at once. The vanilla flavor continued to receive the reverence it deserved until vanilla ice cream was introduced to America in the eighteenth century by Thomas Jefferson. Jefferson had sampled vanilla sweets on a visit to France. He was so impressed by its subtle aromatic flavor that he imported vanilla beans to make an ice cream recipe, which still resides with other historical artifacts in the Library of Congress. It was the popularity of ice cream in 1900s America and, more importantly, the boom of other flavors that sealed the fate of vanilla. Different ice cream textures and flavors, including fruits, nuts, and chocolate, revolutionized the ice cream scene.

In comparison, vanilla ice cream with its colorless, smooth texture was ordinary. This newfound ice cream color palette gave birth to the phrase "plain vanilla," and the moniker stuck. The rest is simply history. Tool #7 is all about embracing the things that are often considered ordinary by comparison. Be Vanilla is a tool that celebrates the simple things that we do to become extraordinary.

What exactly is Tool #7: Be Vanilla all about? To Be Vanilla means building the consistency we talked about in Tool #6 through our routines, systems, and habits. To Be Vanilla is like the foundation of a house. Whether it be for a modest home in Bryan, Texas, or a stately mansion in the Hamptons, building an enduring home requires a strong foundation. Once we have built that firm foundation, all other fixtures and features can be added. Walls can be constructed. Floors can be added, along with appliances, furnishings, a roof, and everything else that rests on top of the foundation. But as important as the foundation is to the structure of the house, it is rarely considered a feature. It may be the most critical part of any house since every other aspect of the house relies on its foundation's stability. Yet it gets very little fanfare or recognition.

Like many of you, I've watched my fair share of real estate and property makeover shows over the years. I have also bought, sold, and improved my own properties. But in all my years, I have never seen or heard of anyone mentioning the foundation as a feature. They may talk about the kitchen, flooring, or even solar panels on the roof, but not the foundation. There are no real estate property listings that quote the thickness and engineering prowess of the foundation. It just doesn't happen. So why is this? Why is the foundation so overlooked? It's simple. Nothing is exciting or cool about a foundation. No matter what additional innovative techniques the builder may have, the foundation has only one role: to provide a firm base for everything else to be built upon. Ever important, but rarely acknowledged–until now. This is the same as our relationship with Tool #7. To Be Vanilla is to build a foundation of routines, systems, and habits for your life and your journey as a leader.

WHAT'S IN A PLAIN NAME?

You may be thinking, *Why is this tool called, Be Vanilla? Why not something else, like "Be Consistent," "Be the Base," or even "Be a Foundation?"* Although I like the rhyming sound of "Be the Base," I called this tool Be Vanilla because, like its namesake, this tool can often be referred to as dull. Telling someone that the only way to become a better leader is through years of positive daily routines and lifelong healthy habits will seldom sound exciting. Also, like the vanilla spice, it's deceptively valuable. As I mentioned before, to Be Vanilla is the main action tool that can help you with all other tools—once it's understood. So its value is immense. And finally, like the humble vanilla bean, getting the desired result takes time, diligence, deliberate actions, and fortitude. There is no shortcut in the process of growing and harvesting the vanilla pod into a usable spice product, and the same is true of this tool.

Whether it's through practicing the 10,000 hours rule or reading books like *Atomic Habits* and *The 7 Habits of Highly Effective People* (one of my all-time favorites), there are many fantastic theories and guidelines for establishing healthy habits in your life. But it doesn't take reading books to understand that our habits impact our lives. A habit is often described as something you regularly or often do, sometimes without knowing, and sometimes it can be hard to stop. We know there are so-called bad habits, like smoking and overeating. We also learn about good habits, like brushing your teeth, wearing a seatbelt, and exercising regularly. Like it or not, these habits, whether good or bad, do impact our lives. The impact can be positive or negative, but there is always an impact.

I did not discover the benefits of adding good habits and routines to my life until I was in my forties. Like everyone, I had formed habits all of my life: some good and some bad. But I didn't understand how to own, control, and use habits for my benefit until I saw one of those viral videos on YouTube. No, not another video of a cat being scared by a cucumber or a dog trying to walk with socks on its feet. This was a video of a 2014 commencement speech given at the University of Texas in Austin by former Navy SEAL Admiral William H. McRaven, who also served as commander of the United States Special Operations Command. In the video, McRaven boldly spoke to the graduating students, parents, faculty, and prestigious alumni. "If you want to change the world, start off by making your bed." His comment was met with polite chuckles, but then he continued:

"If you make your bed every morning, you will have accomplished the first task of the day. It will give you a small sense of pride and will encourage you to do another task, and another, and another. And by the end of the day, that one task completed will have turned into many tasks completed. Making your bed will also reinforce the fact that the little things in life matter. If you can't do the little things right, you'll never be able to do the big things right. And if by chance you have a miserable day, you will come home to a bed that is made. That you made. And a made bed gives you encouragement that tomorrow will be better."

That speech did much more than prompt me to make my bed every day since. McRaven's simple words helped remind me of what I had always instinctively known to be true. If you want to do the big things in life, you must first understand that it starts with the smallest step. His simple, elegant message helped me realize one of the basic principles of Tool #7. You must be intentional when creating positive routines or habits as a tool. I know that sounds simple, but that is the key. As Mr. Ping said to Po in the animated children's classic Kung Fu Panda, "There is no secret ingredient ... To make something special, you just have to believe it's special."

The special ingredient that this tool requires is you. That's why this tool is named Be Vanilla. Like all of the tools in this book, it requires action. But to "be" anything implies a belief in yourself. A belief that you are someone who takes small steps every day. It is about you slowly and methodically taking action to better your life and the lives of those around you. It is about not needing to be recognized for what you do but knowing the value of your stock will grow and reveal itself in time. To Be Vanilla is about you becoming someone who values the little things that eventually lead to accomplishing your goals, big or small.

So how does it work? How do you use Tool #7 in the real world? Yes, Tool #7 is about more than making your bed every day or creating checklists. It's about creating the right habits and processes for yourself, your team, or your family. There is a plethora of great advice on the best ways to form lasting habits. Some common suggestions are to start small, make it simple, and reward yourself when you do well. James Clear, author of *Atomic Habits*, recommends habit stacking, including adding new habits that are somehow associated with others. Over the years, I've found myself trying many techniques with varying degrees of success. But let's face it, good habits are hard to keep. This is why I developed the POC principle as a tool within the tool to help you Be Vanilla.

POC PRINCIPLE

POC is a simple system for achieving your goals, and it stands for Priority, Order, and Consistency. Think of POC as your daily life checklist for getting things done. It reminds us of not only what to do each day but the sequence in which to do it. The POC Principle was partially inspired by a concept known as "big rocks," popularized by Stephen Covey, author of *The 7 Habits of Highly Effective People*. I once saw this "big rocks" theory illustrated by a university professor who started with a large, empty glass jar placed on a table. She then poured sand to fill about one-third of the cylindrical jar, then mentioned that the sand represents the small things in your life. I always imagine small things being the day-to-day tasks in life, like checking emails, sending text messages, scrolling through social media, watching television, and other things that fill our day. The professor then poured a similar amount of pebbles into the crystal-clear jar, which made it easy to distinguish the layer between the sand and the pebbles. In this case, the pebbles were meant to represent the bigger things in life. The pebbles in your life are often the things that you have to do versus the things that you want to do. I envision those pebbles as bills we need to pay, chores that keep our life on track, and other things that are a standard part of modern life. Then, as a final part of the demonstration, she revealed three large rocks and placed them on the table beside the jar. These rocks represent the important things in our lives. These "large rocks" could represent spending time with your family, investing in your personal or career ambition, writing a book, creating a YouTube channel or blog, or whatever the next skill is that you want to grow. These are the things that are truly important in your life. The professor then attempted to place the large, rough stones in the uncovered jar one by one. Since the jar was more than two-thirds full of sand and pebbles, it was a struggle to get the rocks into the jar. Ultimately, after some effort, the "big rocks" rested precariously protruded out from the vase. The big rocks didn't quite fit into the jar, just as they wouldn't "fit" into our lives. The demonstration was meant to show that we often spend so much time on all of the minor things that there's no room for the important things. It is always too late, too hard, requires too much research, or you say, "I'll get to that one day."

    This is where the principle of Priority, Order, and Consistency can help change your life. To continue the big rocks demonstration and ultimately Covey's point, the professor revealed another jar of the same size and shape and began the process of filling the second jar. However, this time the big rocks were added to the jar first. The stones fit securely in the jar with plenty of room to spare. Then the pebbles. They tumbled in and around the stones and filled the large gaps around the stones. Finally, the sand was poured, and the fine grains flowed like currents of water between and around the rocks and pebbles, fitting snugly in the jar. The jar was filled with the same items but with room to spare. I loved this simple demonstration as an analogy for life because the order does matter. It's not enough to simply know your big rocks, your priorities, or your purpose. You must put them first in your life. You must adjust your life around your priorities, not the other way around. Squeezing in your life goals and priorities after everything else is both physically and metaphorically flawed. After applying this "big rocks" concept as a tool in my life for many years, I realized something else was missing. I understood my priorities, but that wasn't enough. I was missing the element of action. More importantly, I was missing a way to act on my priorities regularly. Like many of us, I found myself having ambition but very little energy to accomplish my goals. I was all potential and no kinetic energy. But by combining the concept of Being Vanilla and working on my priorities as a habit, my world began to change. By adding the often-overlooked element of Consistency as part of my playbook, the POC principle was born.

Inserting the element of Consistency as part of striving for your goals adds that all-important rhythm that keeps you moving forward. It's not the big steps; it's the consistent, reliable, regular steps that lead to the vanilla harvest.

A good friend and mentor once described this notion of Being Vanilla, or building habits, as "the drumbeat to the rhythm of life." It was an interesting way to describe how personal routines and habits can help you keep the rhythm of your world. But it wasn't until my son started taking drumming lessons that I understood how true this was. In a band, the drummer keeps the pace and sets the tone for all the musicians. If the drummer is going too fast, the whole band will be rushed. If the drummer is too slow, so is the tempo of the song. But the drummer also helps respond to change. It is not so true for an inexperienced group of would-be musicians like my twelve-year-old son and his bandmates. But if you think about a more established set of musicians, like that of a jazz band, the drummer's job is different. If there's a guitar solo and the guitarist is feeling particularly enthusiastic, the drummer can respond to that energy by keeping the beat, keeping pace, and helping set the tone for the guitarist or any other member of the band. The drummer is like the habits that we form. Habits and rituals need to set the tone, but they also need to respond to change. The formation of new habits is required, or you can ditch old habits that are no longer relevant or productive, given your current life goals.

I've always considered myself a night owl. A typical day for me was to wake up at 7:30 a.m. and be in bed by midnight or 1:00 a.m. This was my sleeping pattern, and it had been this way for most of my adult life. "It is just how my body is wired," I would explain. This sleeping pattern was a part of me. It was a habit. But as I started to strive for new goals in my life but achieved very little progress, I realized something needed to change. Like most of us, there was never enough time in the day, so I decided to create time to work on my goals.

First, I attempted to carve out time each day when I arrived home from the office. But that did not work. I would stay late at a client site or need to run an errand or have that all-important happy-hour drink. There were always life commitments that took priority. I also tried doing things during my lunch break at work. But again, life takes over. I tried many different times, but nothing seemed to stick. My dedicated time was never actually dedicated. I would allow something else to take precedence.

To break the cycle, I decided to carve out two hours in the very early morning. That new morning routine allowed me to do the most important things for a concentrated period of time daily. I now get up at 5:30 a.m. to work on myself. That meant fighting against my old sleeping patterns to create time to think, time to pause, time to spring into action. No matter what I have as an ambition, goal, or personal "big rocks," I find the time in the morning. Little by little, I accomplish those things first, before life takes over. It allows me to pull the things that are most important to me to the front of the queue, and I still do that to this day.

What are your priorities in life? What are you trying to change or accomplish? Maybe it's your ambition to learn a foreign language. Maybe it's to progress in your career. Maybe it's your family. Whatever you decide your most important things are, the things that make the most difference in your life, you must put them first.

You may be thinking, *How can I apply this in my life?* That's a tough one. Our lives are each so different. I can't tell you exactly what to change, but I can tell you how to change. The surest way to accomplish any goal is to take steps every day. Yes, every single day. I know that may sound daunting at first, but it won't be if you start with something simple. As Admiral McRaven elegantly said, "Start off by making your bed."

Perhaps it's not the bed for you. Perhaps it's organizing your office desk each morning or taking a walk every morning before work that leads to a fulfilling sense of accomplishment. To Be Vanilla means creating long-term systems and habits that benefit you, your teams, and everyone around you. By starting small, you are building that foundation from which to expand, to change, and to grow. Just like the vanilla spice, it may take some time to see the fruits of your labor. This growth takes time and patience, and at times it will look and feel like your efforts have made no difference. You may see very little progress or what appears to be nothing at all. But have faith in the system. It will come. Have belief that the process will produce results. Those small steps, your persistence, and fortitude will be rewarded. And like the vanilla farmer, you need to be ready to reap the harvest that will bring value for a lifetime.

IN RETROSPECT

Tool #7—Be Vanilla

- This tool is about building consistency into your life through habits and rituals, which lead to great rewards.
- We learned that producing the vanilla spice takes time and patience; likewise, our goals will take time.
- We talked about starting good habits by beginning with something as simple as making your bed.
- We discovered the principle of POC (Priority, Order, and Consistency) and talked about how to carve out time for your priorities.

Practice Leading by Being Vanilla

1. Make a list of three to five major goals in your life right now. Then, next to each goal, write down when you last worked on it. Have you put those goals in the proper "order" in your life? Set the alarm in the morning one hour earlier than you currently do. Start working on that goal each morning for one month. See what happens to that goal.

2. Make one new positive habit today. If you don't already make your bed every morning, try it. Otherwise, do something physical, like push-ups or sit-ups every day. Build a life full of tiny, positive habits.

"

PROGRESS IS IMPOSSIBLE
WITHOUT CHANGE, AND
THOSE WHO CANNOT
CHANGE THEIR MINDS
CANNOT CHANGE
ANYTHING.

—GEORGE BERNARD SHAW

TOOL #8

Be Agile

What does "agile" mean to you? For me, the first thing that enters my mind is the agility of an incredible animal like the cheetah, the world's fastest land animal and equally nimble, able to turn on a dime in pursuit of its prey. Others will think of superior athletes with incredible speed and remarkable footwork, like soccer legends Cristiano Ronaldo and Lionel Messi. Still, others might think of someone like NBA legend Kobe Bryant, with his ability to move, shake, change direction, and soar through the air. Growing up in Texas, where football is king, my vision of agility was Tony Dorsett and Emmitt Smith of the Dallas Cowboys or Barry Sanders of the Detroit Lions, who amazed me with their ability to move and change direction on the football field. No matter what picture comes into our head, we know that to Be Agile means being nimble, moving quickly and easily, and adapting or responding to the world around us.

Consider Olympic gold medalist Simone Biles, regarded by many to be the greatest gymnast of all time. Biles has over thirty Olympic and World Championship medals and is known for her power, overall athleticism, and difficulty of her moves. Biles is the epitome of strength, grace, and physical agility. Biles' impact and influence on the world of women's gymnastics has been so great that she has the rare distinction of having several gymnastic elements named after her. One on the balance beam, one on the vault, and two on the floor exercise. But one of her signature floor exercise moves was only developed in response to an injury she had at the time of her performance.

During one of her practice sessions, Biles injured her calf muscle. But determined to continue and compete at a world level, Biles and her coach, Aimee Boorman, devised a plan. To minimize the impact on her injured calf, Biles would change the direction of her landing. This was not easy to pull off. The new strategy required Biles to complete a complicated series of floor moves that concluded with a double layout with a half-twist and a blind landing. This slight change allowed Biles to have a front-facing landing with a half layout, which proved to be so unique and tricky to perform that it became one of her signature moves. "The Biles," as it's called in gymnastic circles, was created by turning a point of potential weakness, the injury, into a strength. Moreover, Biles turned the injury into innovation. Biles did not simply survive her circumstances. She was able to assess the situation, make adjustments based on the available information, and thrive. This is what it means to Be Agile; this is what Tool #8 is all about.

I first learned about this tool during my years working in the field of software and technology. In the world of software, there is a project delivery methodology called Agile. Without invoking a collective yawn from all readers of this book, I'll quickly describe the highlights of the method. Agile software delivery was developed in the early 2000s in response to what was perceived as slow, bureaucratic, over-planned, and micromanaged delivery methods. In 2001, a group of software developers from across the US gathered in Snowbird, Utah, to develop a more lightweight, adaptive, and responsive approach to creating and delivering software to customers. This new approach was published as the Manifesto for Agile Software Development and has since become one of the most widely used approaches for software development today.

Agile is designed to help organizations deliver better quality software to customers by promoting incremental product feature delivery. This was a new and somewhat radical approach to creating software previously bound to a monolithic project planning process that would take months or years to complete. The Agile approach promoted a culture of small teams working directly with customers to deliver chunks of working software in short, sharp time blocks called sprints. The customer would then try the features and provide feedback about the software that would allow the team of developers to change and tweak the software before delivering the next version. This test-and-learn sprint cycle would continue every few weeks until the software was ready for release to the general public. This new way of approaching the process was a revolution for both customers and developers and helped usher in a new *current* in the technology sector.

This Agile approach to software delivery and development is comprised of several fundamental values that were adopted as part of the original manifesto designed to help guide would-be

Agilists in ways of thinking differently about the process. Below are the values published as part of the Agile methodology.
- Individuals and interactions over processes and tools
- Working software over comprehensive documentation
- Customer collaboration over contract negotiation
- Responding to change over following a plan

Did you notice the use of the word *over* in the values? You can be forgiven if you did not, but *over* is a vital part of these values. Much like how we use 10LT Tool #1: Purpose "Over" Task, the Agile manifesto authors did not suggest that processes and tools are unnecessary. They are actually confirming the need to consider processes and tools by having them as part of the values. However, given the situation where you have the choice of working closely with someone in your team, you should make *individuals and interactions* a priority *over* focusing on processes and tools. The use of the preposition *over* helps us recognize the choice while allowing us to focus on the right thing.

Contrary to popular belief amongst my fellow tech-heads, the values are not suggesting that we should not do comprehensive documentation. These values, like Purpose Over Task, are designed to help you make better choices and take action on the right things when faced with options. These values are designed to help us think differently about how we see the world around us.

These are all-powerful values that have become the North Star for technologists looking to improve the way they work. But the value that resonates with me the most is the value that states developers should *respond to change over following a plan*. This seems almost obvious as we think about our post-global pandemic world, but as a growing technologist and leader, this thought of adapting to change despite any existing plans was quite liberating at the time. Agile was more than a new way of organizing teams for a software delivery project. It was about a new philosophy for anticipating and managing life's changes.

Agile was more than a move from detailed multipage Gantt charts and project plans to a simple whiteboard with sticky notes. It was a mindset shift. It was a shift from assuming that everything would go according to plan to actively expecting things to change and then adapting when required. In the world of technology, those who chose to adopt Agile were buying into a new approach to rapid decision-making. They were choosing a method that responded to unforeseen circumstances with purpose and intention versus continuing to follow false assumptions with blinders on. Through my experience in this world of software development, I understood the true benefits of using agility as a life and leadership tool.

Tool #8: Be Agile is not about a software development methodology or the ability to outmaneuver linebackers on a football field. It is not about having the dexterity to perform somersaults or a double layout. So what does it truly mean to Be Agile for your family or as a leader? First, let's start with a concept known by psychologists as cognitive agility. Cognitive agility is a skill used to help people perform well during rapidly changing situations.

Whether it is a challenge in the office, on the sports field, at home, or due to an unforeseen pandemic, we need to respond to dynamic situations and help make the right decisions. These decisions, driven by continual real-time change, uncertainty, and ambiguity, are labeled dynamic decision-making. Traditional decision-making, which is the opposite, requires a single binary decision, like turning left or right to reach your destination. Our complex lives and changing environments require many context-driven, small, interdependent choices based on the often-evolving situation. You can think of these decisions more like an internal navigation system that recalculates the route based on your current speed, mode of transportation, current location, and changing traffic conditions. Dynamic decision-making has typically been studied in high-stress professions like fighter pilots, surgeons, and firefighters. However, in today's world, the practice of dynamic decision-making has become more and more commonplace across a variety of professions and settings, especially for leaders. This means that although the risk is usually not a matter of life and death, the skills associated with cognitive agility can serve to help everyday leaders manage the barrage of daily pressures and decisions required by mothers, fathers, students, and managers.

In the research paper by Dr. Darren Good and Dr. Bauback Yeganeh titled "Cognitive Agility: Adapting to Real-time Decision Making at Work," they provide a framework for thinking with agility. The framework suggests that cognitive agility is the ability a person has to move their thinking and reasoning flexibly between openness and focus. Their research states:

> "A dynamic, information-rich environment requires being able and willing to seek out new information. Yet continually paying attention to new information will eventually lead to distraction. Focused attention, on the other hand, is also vital, since depth of information can be critical to successful task accomplishment. Yet too much focus will lead to missing important information in

a changing context. Gathering new information (i.e., openness) and sticking to a coherent cognitive thread (i.e., focus) are both essential for success in such an environment. Therefore, an individual must be able to flexibly use openness and focus according to the shifting needs of the environment."

When I try to explain this concept to others, I like to have them picture sliders on an audio mixing board. I think of a music producer or sound engineer using similar slides to finely tune and mix the many parts of a song. They mix the singer's vocals and band instruments to make the music track just right. If the signer's voice is too prominent, that slider is turned down. If the music is not loud enough, that slider is moved up. The music producer uses what they hear to make adjustments on the spot. We can think of ourselves as the producer of our world, dialing up or down the various aspects of agility like openness, flexibility, and focus, to resolve each challenge as it comes.

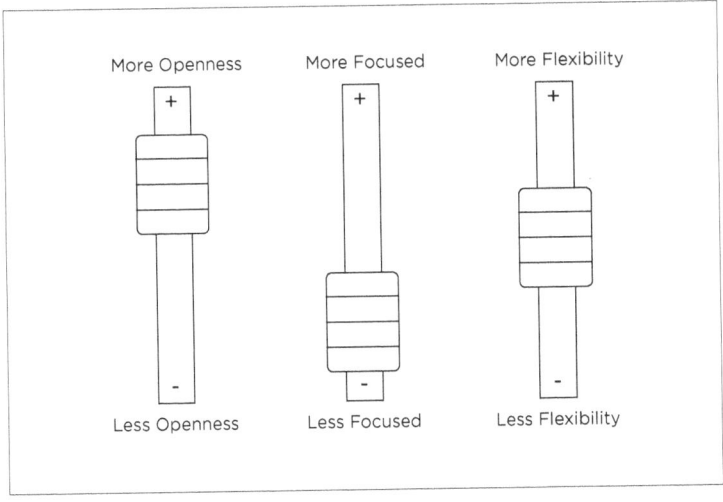

Fig. 3 Cognitive Agility diagram.

To Be Agile in the context of Tool #8 builds on this construct of openness, flexibility, and focus well beyond a dynamic decision framework. To use agility as a tool in life or as a leader is to adopt a personal position that can successfully navigate life's many challenges, changes, failures, and disappointments.

Some days, some weeks, and some months life sucks. Let's face it; life is not always predictable. Things will go wrong, and we will have trials that will challenge our resolve. Yes, even as we embrace the benefits of creating consistency through positive habits and routines, as we discussed in Tool #7, we should not confuse consistency with certainty. Consistency is about methodically aligning our actions with the things that give us purpose. But to Be Vanilla does not mean creating certainty or avoiding change. I would argue that it is just the opposite. To Be Vanilla in parts of our lives allows us to effectively respond to the unexpected. That consistency becomes a solid base or platform from which we can respond to any situation. It helps us be more Agile.

Let's think back to the agility of gymnast Simone Biles in developing one of her signature moves. After the unfortunate and unplanned circumstance of the calf injury, she had to be open to considering all of her available options. Should she stop competing to allow time for additional healing of the injury? Or should she continue to work around the issue? Once listening to and considering all of the options, she had to have the flexibility to work through the various pros, cons, and benefits. Then Biles and her coach would have distilled the options and begun to focus on the most appropriate approach given the information at hand. But think about Biles and her situation. She had the added advantage of having an incredible base to build from. If she was not already an accomplished gold medalist and able to consistently perform the floor exercises at a world-class level, making an unprecedented alteration to a standard move may not have been an option. But they made the front-facing landing decision based on everything they knew about the sport, the impact of her injury, and Biles's exceptional athleticism. Although I am sure she would have tried and failed many times in the attempt to perfect *The Biles*, she ultimately made a bold decision resulting from her ability to Be Agile.

Are you Agile? Are you set in your ways, or are you open to new ideas? Do you look for new opinions and perspectives, or are you simply seeking those voices that validate your own? Are you easily overwhelmed by information and choices, or are you able to focus on one step at a time? Are you comfortable failing and making mistakes, or are you paralyzed by the fear of making the wrong decision? It is the fear and shame associated with failure that can prevent our ability to Be Agile. Fear can block our ability to be open and flexible. Fear can center our focus on the wrong things.

FEAR OF FAILURE

My wife told me a story of her first time being gripped by the fear of failure. She was really into the sport of BMX bike racing as a young girl. This was a great sport for her and offered lots of opportunities to work off her high-energy personality. It was also fun because she realized quite early that she was as good as any boy on the track. One Saturday morning in June, seven-year-old Jillian found herself in one of the big local championship races for her age group. She was full of excitement and confidence as she sat on her bike with one foot at the starting line.

As the starting gun sounded, she was off like a rocket, leaving a cloud of dust in her wake. Maneuvering the hills, the mud, and the corners, she raced, feeling on top of the world. She was not only competing with the boys on this day, but she was winning. She bolted well ahead of the pack. Then things suddenly changed: the fear of failure took over. She had never been the leader on the track before and started to question which direction the track was going. She began to question whether she was going the right way. And with that lingering doubt, she decided to slow down to let the second-place rider catch her and ultimately pass her. She was more comfortable relying on the judgment of others to lead the way for her. It was a pivotal moment in her childhood, and she remembers that decision to fall back to this day. She was more afraid of leading and failing than trusting her gut and winning. Jillian finished the race in a respectable fourth place, but the fear of failure was too strong.

Are you afraid of taking the wrong path? What would have happened if she had not talked herself into settling? Are you rolling through all of the reasons why you shouldn't do something? Ask yourself, "Am I afraid to fail?" Or do you fear the ridicule of others? Our challenge as leaders is to learn how to overcome the fear of failure or at least the fear of being ashamed to experience failure in our hunt for success.

In the animal kingdom, the ability to change, adapt, and react can be the difference between life and death. Cheetahs are solitary hunters, so agility and speed are their primary weapons in their quest to feed themselves and their families. But in the wild, the cheetah does not get to choose a life that is lined with an easy food source. They commonly seek to dine on other equally agile wildlife, like gazelles, impalas, springbok, and other antelope. But being the fastest land animal on Earth does not guarantee success. Remember what we learned in Tool #6 about the cheetah? The nimble cheetah will often use its superior speed and the element of surprise when pursuing a fleet-footed gazelle, but the cheetah will only be able to have its pedal to the floor for a few hundred yards before requiring a rest (pulse). That means if the gazelle can dodge and weave through the grassy landscape for a few hundred yards, it can survive.

A study of wild cheetah pursuits showed that of 192 hunts, the cheetah was only successful 58 percent of the time. That means the fastest animal in the world, with its superior stealth and agility, fails in almost half of its pursuits. So what does this mean to us? What does the apparently ineffective hunting practices of the cheetah teach us as people, as leaders? It teaches us that even one of the most evolved, finely tuned hunting machines ever to walk the Earth experiences failure, and I mean lots of failures, and we will fail too.

One of the apex predator's secrets to evolutionary dominance is its ability to bounce back from apparent failure to achieve hunting glory. The cheetah has learned to manage failure during its many pursuits to achieve ultimate success. I can imagine the cheetah hates failing to catch its prey, as any of us would. The cheetah has no choice but to shake off the past and, yes, try again or die. Through the evolutionary process, you and I no longer need to hunt for survival. But our world is more like life in the wild than we'd like to admit. We cannot control everything in our world, so this ability to pivot and thrive through success and failure becomes an essential skill.

Being an Agile leader is about learning how to make the best of any situation by considering the current context. Each move, each decision is based on your current position. It is based on the information at hand. To Be Agile is to know that although our plans are often linear, our journey through life and as leaders is littered with twists and turns. Each right or wrong decision, each opportunity or mistake is part of the journey. Embrace the challenge of your next hunt, race, or project without fear.

VISION AND REVISION

Another way to think about Being Agile as a leader is to think about the two major stages in the process. I like to call these stages *vision* and *revision*. In summary, vision is where you want to go, the goal you're trying to achieve, or the plan. Our challenge as leaders is to keep ourselves and those around us working toward the vision. This vision is not necessarily some grand vision. This can be for solving any problem, large or small, or reaching any goal. When faced with a problem or challenge, you continually ask yourself, "What is the vision or goal?" Moving on, the next stage is revision.

Revision is typically described as the act of revising. To revise is to change, adjust, or amend something, especially in the light of further information or evidence. This is how modern leaders become Agile. Agile leaders strive to thrive in times of revision. When others insist on blocking out new ideas, an Agile leader knows when to be open to unique and diverse opinions.

They also have an aptitude that allows them to move into action. They know how to distill the inputs quickly and without being overwhelmed with data—making decisions and taking action toward the vision with the required flexibility and focus.

Yes, like the bulk of the tools included in 10LT, an element of action is required to truly experience the benefits. To Be Agile is more than being open, flexible, and focused. To transcend from simply having cognitive agility to being an Agile leader, Tool #8 demands applying what we know. An Agile leader also has the ability to act based on the information at hand.

One of my favorite techniques for using agility is the decision cycle developed by Colonel John Boyd of the US Air Force. The cycle was designed as a framework for decision-making, especially when there is a competitive or real-time need for working through decisions. Boyd's system is affectionately known as an "OODA Loop" (pronounced like food-uh without the f) and contains four distinct parts: Observe, Orient, Decide, and Act. Boyd's method of continuous looping through these stages is designed to give an advantage to fighter pilots during the heat of combat.

The cycle suggests that pilots or anyone can gain an advantage over their adversaries or the competition by continually cycling through the states faster than others. Observation is about scanning the situation, and orientation is about making adjustments based on the observable environment. The fighter pilot makes a context-driven decision, then acts on that decision. The "loop" then continues until a victory or loss is achieved. Okay, confession. Yes, Boyd's simple steps are a great way to help you to think and act Agile. But I must admit that part of my love for this model is how easily the phrase slips off the tongue. Since I first discovered Boyd's approach, I just loved saying OODA Loop. Try saying it three times in a row without smiling. It's another tool within a tool that can help leaders, teams, families, and organizations think, act, and become more Agile.

I know that some of you are thinking, "TMI, KG. I hear you saying a lot about agility, but what's in it for me? What can I do to Be Agile?" So below, I've summarized the three key points.

1. Being Agile is a mindset. It starts by allowing yourself to think differently about every situation. An Agile leader sees opportunity where others see obstacles. An Agile leader loves a plan but plans to change. Like many other tools, you get better and more skilled at wielding the device the more you practice.

2. Open yourself up to more. Open yourself to more voices that are not like yours. Open yourself up to hearing and considering different views without judgment. As Mark Twain said, "It ain't what you don't know that gets you into trouble. It's what you know for sure that just ain't so." Free yourself to learn new things from other backgrounds and ethnicities. Allow yourself to be open, observe, and fully orient yourself to others with empathy, but keep your focus on the end goal.

3. Act and assess constantly. Take action and be prepared to adjust and rework as needed.

To Be Agile means having a complete understanding that life is not always as predictable as we hoped it to be. To Be Agile is to build a life, a team, and a family with a certain amount of resilience and tolerance for the unexpected.

IN RETROSPECT

Tool #8—Be Agile

- This tool is about thinking differently with openness and without fear of failure to solve problems and make decisions.
- Being an Agile leader is about learning how to make the best of any situation by considering the current context.
- We learned about the Agile movement that started in software development and its role in business.
- We saw how Being Agile helped Simone Biles work around an injury to create something unique and special.
- We learned that applying agility through cognitive agility is the combination of openness, focus, and flexibility.
- We talked about the fear of failure.
- We also learned about the OODA Loop as another tool for rapid decision-making.

Practice Leading by Being Agile

1. Make a list of your three most important goals. Think about how you can start working on one of them today. Be intentional with your Agile thinking and begin without knowing everything—start small. Use openness and flexibility to cycle through solutions to each problem or issue. Force yourself to be okay with not knowing all the answers. Be okay with making a mistake. Focus on each task at hand, knowing the unanswered questions will be answered later.

2. Reflect on the last five major decisions you had to make. Look at various situations in the office, with the kids, regarding financial decisions, helping a friend, or anything else where a decision was needed. Now reflect on the amount of Agility you think you used for each decision. Were you open? Were you able to focus as needed? Were you flexible and adaptive to the context? Did you take action?

> TRUST IS THE HIGHEST FORM OF HUMAN MOTIVATION. IT BRINGS OUT THE VERY BEST IN PEOPLE.
>
> —STEPHEN R. COVEY

TOOL #9

Be Real

"My father was a foreman for a construction company and died in an accident a few years ago." This is what I told the other kids at school whenever someone asked about my father as I was growing up. I'm not sure how many times I told that story to my classmates or the teachers, but it was not true. From what I know, he was a construction worker in the 1970s. That part is true, but the rest of what I know is sketchy at best. The truth is that I simply do not know what happened to my father or why I never heard from him after the age of six or seven. Even those details are a bit fuzzy as I write this book, since neither my mother nor I can genuinely recall when I saw my father for the last time or why it was the last time.

Over the years, my memory of him and his face have become a blur, but that faded memory is all I have. In my head, I see a tall, dark, handsome man with smooth chocolate skin, a slight afro hidden under a wide-brimmed cowboy hat, and a bushy Burt Reynolds mustache. I don't have a photo of him, so my memory is likely a mixture of truth, fiction, and hope. I feel embarrassed by the words on this page. It is hard for me to think that I was so ashamed of my personal truth as a youth that I resorted to such a tragic tale. For that, I am truly sorry. I can only guess that the story I told until I was a pre-teen was easier than answering with the truth. Saying my dad died in an accident stopped people from asking more questions. It halted the conversation and allowed me to quickly move back to being semi-normal compared to my friends and classmates, who had plenty of great dad stories to share. It was an easier answer to a hard question for a kid trying to fit in. After all, my inner dialog at the time must have convinced me that I was the only one in that situation.

I'm not sure when I became brave enough to simply answer the questions about my father with "I don't know," but I can only imagine the moment was both nerve-racking and liberating. Even today, although more than forty-five years have passed, I still don't have an elegant, nonchalant, conversational answer to the seemingly innocent statement, "Tell me about your father."

For me, it was my imperfect knowledge of my father. For others, it may be an imperfect childhood or imperfect relationship or imperfect education credentials or an imperfect criminal record or an imperfect credit score or an imperfect marriage or imperfect kids. Whatever it is for you, the wave of shame is still the same. It has become easier for me over the years. I now stick to an answer that I can authentically stand behind: "I don't know" or "I'm not sure." It's not a perfect answer or a perfect situation. Only after learning the right tools did I start to understand the value of my uniqueness. I started appreciating this and all of the other imperfections that have served to shape me and help me become the real KG.

THE CRACKS

Nowhere is this concept of valuing imperfections better illustrated than with the ancient Japanese art form called Kintsugi. This is the centuries-old tradition of repairing accidentally broken pottery with lacquer and gold. The golden joinery is used as a way to celebrate the cracks or imperfections in the ceramic instead of hiding or obscuring them. Legend has it that the tradition began when Japanese shogun Ashikaga Yoshimasa accidentally dropped and broke his favorite Chinese tea bowl in the late fifteenth century. The dish had broken into pieces, so in desperation to salvage the damaged bowl, he sent the pottery back to China for repairs. However, when the much-anticipated repaired tea bowl arrived, it was fixed with a series of unsightly metal staples to bind the cracks.

Displeased with the outcome of the repair to his favorite vessel, Yoshimasa then commissioned his craftsmen to devise a more aesthetically pleasing means of repair. The craftsmen agonized for days over better ways and methods that could be used to elegantly reassemble the bowl pieces. Finally, they had their answer. Instead of attempting to disguise the repaired cracks, they decided to highlight these areas with a gold solution. The tea bowl glued together at its veins of damage by gold was far more beautiful than the shogun could have imagined. The tea bowl became a treasured art piece, and the tradition of Kintsugi was born. As Ernest Hemingway said, "The world breaks everyone, and afterwards many are strong at the broken places."

Kintsugi is a wonderful metaphor for us as people and leaders since we are all shaped by both favor and flaw. This concept of learning to appreciate and even cherish our failures, frailties, and times when we have been broken is only one aspect of Tool #9, Be Real.

In the world of computer technology, there is a coding practice called WYSIWYG, pronounced "wiz-ee-wig." Yes, this is another cool rhyme-time word that I often say three times in a row to brighten my day, but again, I digress. WYSIWYG is an acronym for "what you see is what you get." This coding practice, first popularized in the late 1970s, allows developers to edit code in a form that closely resembles its appearance when displayed to the end-user. It was introduced to enable the developer to align more closely with the customer while creating the product or web page. And when it comes to Tool #9: Be Real, this is exactly who we should be as leaders. Our default position should be, "What you see is what you get." Tool #9 is centered on creating connections to others through authenticity.

I'll be upfront with you. Like Tool #3: Tell Different Stories, this tool is another hard one for me, and I suspect the same is true for many others who read these pages. This tool is about each of us taking a moment to acknowledge the journey that we have been on. At times, it takes bravery. At times, it takes vulnerability. It requires us to realize that our unique journey is what makes our next steps possible. However winding the road has been, the path has intersected with this moment to help you take your next steps. Our journey as a leader had to include some good days and bad days to make us resilient. Our failures have helped us create our own psychological tools and solutions. Our bumps and bruises and frailties have helped us connect to those around us on a human level.

Okay, okay. I know there is a lot to think about for Being Real, so let's simplify things. If I were to give you the elevator pitch on what Tool #9 boils down to, I would say this, "Being Real is about creating connections through transparency and trust." It's that simple.

Transparency is about offering to let other people into your world to see the authentic leader you are, see the real person you are, and allowing others to understand your journey as a leader. It is similar to Tool #3 in that this tool is intended to help provide context and connection with those around us. This transparency forces us to be more open and honest with the source of our thinking and to be more vulnerable at times.

I remember when I was attending primary school as a kid, I began to get more and more confident in mathematics. As I had started feeling more confident, I would work out most of the equations in my head and simply write the resulting answer on the homework or exam. I was not perfect but would typically score 80 to 90 percent or better on most assignments, so I was quite pleased with myself. After a few weeks of what I considered one of my strongest subjects in school, I remember my teacher calling me up to her desk. She said, "Kerry, I've asked you a few times to start showing your work, but you aren't doing it; what's going on?" To which I timidly replied, "I don't know, Miss Blackstone. It's just easier and faster to work it out in my head." She then said, "I can see you're smart and can work out most things in your head." No one aside from my mother had ever told me that I was smart, so needless to say, I was already hooked by what she had to say. Miss Blackstone continued, "But I know there are some areas where you are struggling, Kerry, especially around the harder, more complex equations. If you don't show me your work and what you are thinking, I can't help you get better. I want to help you be your best."

Being transparent is equivalent to showing your work and being open to potential critique and criticism. By exposing our thinking and becoming more vulnerable, we can often find the answers we need. One of my favorite authors, Brené Brown, loosely describes vulnerability as uncertainty and emotional exposure in her books *Daring Greatly* and *Dare to Lead*. Brown, a fellow Texan, also talks about vulnerability requiring courage, and the same is true for Being Real and transparent. But while Brown touts the benefits of being vulnerable as people and leaders, she also says, "Vulnerability without boundaries is not vulnerability." No, Being Real is not about oversharing intimate secrets or negative information with your family or team to simply get it off your chest. No, I did not create Tool #9 as some "code" for a therapy session or a personal confessional.

Transparency, vulnerability, and Being Real require openness, but within boundaries and in the appropriate context. Transparency is keeping your team informed as the latest changes in corporate structure are occurring. It is letting them know that you don't have all of the answers but are committed to letting them know more as you know more. Being Real is admitting to your young adult daughter that you also made some bad relationship moves in your youth. Being Real is confessing to your colleagues that you discovered a significant calculation error in the report you distributed last week. Being Real is letting yourself off the hook from attempting to be perfect. Like many of you know and others will come to know, being a leader often comes with some perceived pressure. We can feel the pressure to know all of the answers, the pressure to always be in control, the pressure to get it right every time. You can use Tool #9 as your official pressure relief valve.

To Be Real is a surefire way to relieve yourself of the burden of being perfect because that's not what it means to be a leader. Being a transparent leader is about "showing your work" while resolving the challenges and complexities of life. But just like showing your work in mathematics, this can also allow others in. You are letting others in on what you are thinking, what you are imagining, or why you are contemplating certain decisions. This openness also allows for a two-way exchange of information and ideas. It allows others to contribute to your leader's journey. It helps others do what Miss Blackstone did for me—help me be my best. This idea of transparency can help the looping monologue in your head become a conversation of clarity.

TWO-WAY TRUST

This two-way exchange of ideas and context sharing helps create trust between people, which, along with transparency, is the other aspect of Tool #9 that you should remember. I was once told a story of trust that helps illustrate this concept perfectly. Many years ago, in a small town outside New England, there lived a baker and a farmer. The baker had been purchasing a pound of butter from the farmer for months to help make his cakes, loaves of bread, and treats. One day the baker decided to check to see if the farmer was truly providing a pound of butter. The baker weighed the butter, and sure enough, it was less than a pound. Furious with the thought that the farmer had been ripping the baker off for months, the baker decided to take the farmer to court. The baker presented the case to the judge. Then the judge asked the farmer how the farmer had been measuring the pound of butter. The farmer replied, "I had never considered that the pound was not a pound, your honor. I have been purchasing a pound loaf of bread from the baker each morning for years, and I only own a scale to measure what I give to the baker. I take the one-pound loaf of bread each morning and put it on one side of my scale, and then I measure an equal amount of butter to give to the baker. If anyone is to be blamed, it is the baker." The moral of this simple story is that trust is both given and earned by both parties in any relationship. The same applies to leaders, teams, and our families.

Yes, to Be Real as a leader is about transparency, authenticity, integrity, character, vulnerability, truth, and trust. Yes, the answer to this proverbial life test is: "D, all of the above." Why, you may ask? Because we want to trust our leaders. I often hear the comment, "Leaders should be held to a higher standard," but I don't buy into that theory. I believe these are simply human standards, and we yearn for these standards in hopes of trusting the people in our lives or those who impact our lives. We long to live in a world where we can trust others. To Be Real as a leader can be one of many ways to build trust with others.

TRUST MATTERS

There are many research papers and studies that suggest that trust matters in the context of our career or business. In one study, Kurt Dirks and Donald Ferrin collected research on trust in leadership from over four decades of data. Their research shows that where there was trust in a leader, employees were less likely to resign from their job. They believe the information from their leaders more, and more importantly, they commit to company decisions more. This same desire to trust exists equally in the context of our family and our community. The good news is that you already have the tools needed to build trust. There is evidence of this in other research by John Zenger and Joseph Folkman, authors of *Speed: How Leaders Accelerate Successful Execution*, who uncovered three key elements that were often the foundations of trust. Zenger and Folkman found that positive relationships, good judgment, and consistency have the most impact on trust. We learned how to connect with others and build those positive relationships through Tool #3: Tell Different Stories. We have explored how to make better decisions in Tool #8: Be Agile. We have also studied the benefits of consistency and how to Be Vanilla in Tool #7. In their Harvard Business Review article, Zenger and Folkman state:

> "We also found that level of trust is highly correlated with how people rate a leader's overall leadership effectiveness...We were also curious to know if leaders needed to be skilled in all three elements to generate a high level of trust and whether any one element had the most significant impact on the trust rating. To gauge this, we created an experiment where we separated leaders into high and low levels on each of the three pillars and then measured the level of trust. Intuitively we thought that consistency would be the most important element. Saying one thing and doing another seems like it would hurt trust the most. While our analysis showed that inconsistency does have a negative im-

pact (trust went down 17 points), it was relationships that had the most substantial impact. When relationships were low and both judgment and consistency were high, trust went down 33 points. This may be because many leaders are seen as occasionally inconsistent. We all intend to do things that don't get done, but once a relationship is damaged or if it was never formed in the first place, it's difficult for people to trust."

Again, it is about the connections we create as leaders that have the most impact.

No matter the setting, we crave the same thing from our leaders. We simply want to trust them. Trust them to guide us, trust them to believe in us, or simply trust them to be a shoulder to lean on. To be transparent and connected through trust is Being Real. To Be Real is to allow more people to see us for who we are, both good and bad. To Be Real is to gain trust through our connections with others. Tool #9 is equally about seeing those around us with veins of gold, knowing that perfection is not the goal. The goal is to know that we are all bruised and broken in different ways. To Be Real is to use those flaws in the most positive way humanly possible. To Be Real is to no longer hide who we are but to reveal who we are in ways that can help others.

To Be Real is like other tools in this book. The notion of Being Real should be a familiar concept to most of us. Again, this tool is not new. Although my hope is that these words help remind some of you about the ways to use what is already a part of us. Like Being Vanilla, this is another tool that allows us to change everything by changing very little. This tool begs us to simply be open to showing who we are in more ways and in more situations.

But as with many things in life, some of you will still treat these tools as things on your to-do list, and that's okay. It's the inherent flaw with numbering the tools in the way that I have. Some of you will be thinking, *I have now learned almost all of the tools. I'm good to go, KG.* Even if you do treat them as a list, don't fall into the trap of ticking off each tool as accomplished, as done, as finished. I know I've mentioned it before, but it is worth saying again. These are not tricks or items on a checklist to fast-track your leadership journey. These are intended to be tools to live by.

These are tools you will use for a lifetime, and that is what is so powerful about tools. The good ones are enduring. They have lasting power and can be helpful even as we gain in skill or learn new and better tools. Like a tradesman, you need to continue to perfect your skills, and these tools will help you along the way. You cannot short-circuit the process. Knowing the tool and recognizing its value is part of the process. Another is discovering how to be bold and fashion the tools to fit your style, approach, and personality.

IN RETROSPECT

Tool #9—Be Real

- This tool is about authenticity and leveraging the good and bad parts of our lives to help others.
- We learned to celebrate flaws through the ancient Japanese artform of Kintsugi.
- We talked about Being Real as a way to "show your work" and how we are thinking as leaders.
- We learned the importance of leading with trust.

Practice Leading by Being Real

1. Try sharing a like-for-like story with your team the next time there is a situation of uncertainty. If there is a restructure in the company, share how you have been through similar challenges in your career. If it is a low-revenue month, mention how you have dealt with this challenge in your personal or work life. If the corporate political scene is particularly toxic, talk about your experiences with another organization. It doesn't matter the situation; try to reveal more of the Real you with each interaction.

2. Over the next two weeks, "show your work" by letting others know what you think. Whenever you find yourself giving instructions or a solution to others, expand the conversation with how you arrived at that answer. Use the phrase, "My thinking was . . ." to let others in on how or why you take a specific position.

3. Take a moment to tackle any unresolved personal truths. This Saturday, give yourself two hours of me-time. Do

something mildly physical like a long, slow walk or driving the car. Reflect on the world you have created, and confront any personal parts of your story that have yet to be told. Be honest with yourself first. Once you can be okay with being imperfect, you will be okay allowing others to see you with cracks mended with gold.

CONTINUE TO BE BOLD, COURAGEOUS. TRY TO CHOOSE THE WISEST THING AND ONCE YOU'VE CHOSEN THE WISEST THING, GO OUT AND TRY TO ACHIEVE IT. BE IT.

—MAYA ANGELOU

TOOL #10

Be Bold

THE ROAD TO AUGUSTA: STEPPING FORWARD

Circling back to this story I began earlier in the book; I'll tell you how it ended. The traffic seemed to stretch for miles in an instant. The accident was only seconds ago, but dozens of faceless people were already ogling from their cars as they slowly drove past the wreckage to get to their next task. Others had stopped their cars, SUVs, and pickup trucks where they were in the hope of offering help. Some called 911, and other bystanders just wanted to compare stories.

"Did you see that?"

"Oh my God! It was just rolling and flipping and rolling."

"I don't think anyone could survive that!"

"He almost hit us. I can't believe it missed us."

My older brother, Rick, and I were amongst that cohort of people wondering what could be done to help. The battered truck sat teetering on its side, and no one knew exactly what to do. But as we all gathered to bear witness to the accident, the situation changed in the blink of an eye.

The truck started to emit smoke from the crushed engine. The smoke then turned to licks of fire. It went from a flicker to a steady orange, then to a small but true white-hot flame before our eyes. I had no time to second-guess myself. I'm not sure who stepped forward first, Rick or me, but we were both rushing toward the flames before we knew it. The problem with that was that we didn't know exactly why. The driver could have been thrown free from the truck during the violence of its flipping end-over-end. Yet we continued forward. It wasn't quite like you see in the heroic scenes of the cinema, but you get my drift. The flames were small but growing by the second. The fire seemed to have two paths: one toward the mangled rear of the truck and another from the engine. The engine fire enveloped the hood without notice, but all we could think was that maybe he was still in there.

"Is anybody in there?" a voice shouted from the roadside.

"Is he okay?" asked another voice.

Rick and I didn't even speak; we just started doing. We did whatever felt right. I pulled unsuccessfully at the door of the sideways cabin. The door was facing straight up to the blue sky, but the result was the same. I pulled and pulled, but nothing happened. It was too warped and mangled to budge.

"Do you see him?" shouted Rick.

"No, I don't see him!" I said with a strained and breathless voice as I looked through the rear window. I didn't see him in the cabin. "That's good," I said as I considered the alternative. A sudden sigh of relief came over me.

"Where is he?" Rick asked.

"Does anyone see the driver?" I shouted at the other bystanders. We could finally hear the sirens of the emergency vehicles coming in the distance, but we couldn't wait for them to arrive. The wreckage continued to get hotter with the growing flames.

Maybe it was because we saw it happening from the start. Maybe it was because no one else moved forward. Maybe it was because any life is a life worth saving. Whatever the reason, we were determined to find the driver. Other witnesses and bystanders started looking around the wreckage site amongst the ankle-high weeds and debris scattered for yards along the highway and the grassy median.

"Hello! Can you hear us?" I called. "Does anyone see him yet?" I yelled to anyone who was able to hear me. The driver was nowhere to be found. Not thrown from the truck during the crash and not inside the truck's squashed cabin. It didn't make sense. The driver couldn't have just vanished. With every second that passed, panic started setting in.

We heard voices saying, "Move back. It's going to explode." Another voice simply said, "Lord, help him! Lord help his soul."

The fire was growing stronger. The smoke was now billowing through the engine, and Rick decided to take a closer look through the mangled truck's cabin window. "I see a shirt. I see him!" Rick shouted.

Sure enough, as I kneeled to look closer through the still-closed windows, there it was, a plaid shirt tucked neatly in the slither of space between the seat and the steering wheel. The driver was still in the crushed and battered truck. Even as the vehicle lay partially on its side, gravity had not dislodged him from the floorboard. We found him. But then came the realization that there was no way to reach him. The doors couldn't be opened, but we had to get in. Rick once again pulled at the door in desperation while I started kicking at the back window. At first, nothing happened. The toughened glass showed no signs of budging. *Thump, thump, thump* sounded, as the most powerful kicks with the soles of my Timberland boots met the glass with no effect on the wreck's unyielding window.

My heart sank as I thought about the reality of the situation. We were stuck. We had all of the best intentions to help, but he was going to die. We could no longer risk our own lives if there was no hope of saving someone we did not even know. The unfathomable truth started to sink in. This man was going to burn to death, separated only by a pane of glass.

No, no, no! That can't be true. This can't end like this! I thought and began to kick again. I then said to my brother, "One, two, kick!" as he acknowledged my cue. We began to kick the glass in unison and with a steely determination this time. "One, two, kick! One, two, kick! One, two, kick!" The crash sounded out, and it was the most relieving noise I'd heard in ages. The glass shattered into thousands of pieces. The glass that remained around the edge of the cabin was razor-sharp, but we had no time to worry about that kind of detail. We both reached into the smoky cabin and tugged at the clothes that we could grasp. With a handful of the torn sleeves and tattered pants in our tight grips, we dislodged him from the floorboards. His limp body lay now within reach, so we pulled him by the arms and legs to get him out of the truck. There was no movement from him. His body was limp and pliable as we carried his mangled frame across the median to safety. After that, everything was a blur. I'm not sure if the paramedics were already on the scene or who performed

CPR, but he was out of the burning heap of wreckage, and that's all I can remember.

I learned a lot that day. But what I learned had nothing to do with me. What I learned was that we, all of us, have an incredible capacity inside of us. I know it sounds like a cliché, but it is true. I learned that life is too precious and fragile to waste. I learned that no matter who we are or where we are on our journey, we can have an impact. I learned that through action, things can change. I learned that anything is possible once you take a step forward. That day, I started to understand the value of Tool #10: Be Bold.

What does the word "bold" mean to you? Do you think of a person being audacious, confident, or brave? Or do you think of less flattering traits like being loud, pushy, or brazen? Or does the word only represent the thickened typeface of your favorite font? Frankly, it was the latter for me until I started to understand the benefits of Being Bold in my life. Yes, the keyboard shortcut Ctrl + B, the way to make a word stand out in a document, was the only boldness that I experienced for much of my adult life. I never considered Being Bold because I considered it a trait for other people. I considered Being Bold a personality type, like being outgoing, confident, or outspoken. If you had asked me to describe myself in twenty words or less, or even one hundred words, the word "bold" would have never entered my mind as a self-description. However, as I started my journey as a leader, I soon realized the importance of leading with boldness as a tool.

It is this ability to Be Bold as a leader that I want to explore as the last tool in 10LT. First, let's get to the heart of the matter and talk about the definition of bold. What does it mean? What is Being Bold in the context of a growing leader? According to the *Oxford Dictionary*, "bold" is defined as "a person, action, or idea showing a willingness to take risks; confidence, and courage." Yes, to Be Bold takes courage, just like some of the other tools we've already explored, like Telling Different Stories, Creating Currents, Being Agile, and Being Real. So what does it mean to Be Bold in the context of 10LT? In short, to Be Bold is to adopt a personal posture of courage and calculated confidence in your actions. To Be Bold means speaking up when others will not. To Be Bold means making the decision that has to be made when you don't want to make it. To Be Bold means taking action instead of merely resting on the fence. It does not mean being reckless or arbitrary in your decisions. It is just the opposite. Foolishness is not considering the risks. Bold is considering the risks but taking a calculated step forward based on the information available.

Just like the frameworks for decisions required to Be Agile, to Be Bold takes an openness to consider all of the available inputs, including potential risks and rewards. It also takes action. Bold leaders act with clarity; those without boldness continue to weigh their options. To Be Bold in the context of this book means permitting yourself to use the tools you have and continually taking steps forward. Yes, to Be Bold means actively using the tools from 10LT and then integrating some of your own into your personal toolbelt. To Be Bold requires you to make some mistakes but be brave enough to try again. Remember: To Be Bold isn't about always making the *right* decision; it is about making *a* decision, though. Boldness implies you have a choice as well as a voice. To

Be Bold is to align these two. This tool is about no longer being a bystander in your life but instead taking steps forward to live it with intention. As Solomon Northup said in his memoir, which inspired the Oscar-winning film *12 Years A Slave*, "I don't want to survive. I want to live." To Be Bold is to live.

BOLD MOVES

Research by management consulting firm McKinsey & Company found that boldness has a significant benefit in the corporate world—after they compared thousands of companies. Organizations that make bold moves thrive, while others merely survive or die. The article "Bold Moves Are Less Risky Than a Timid Corporate Strategy" explains the benefits of businesses making bold moves and shows the success organizations have had over a ten-year period, such as Corning Inc, Canadian National Railway, Burberry, and dozens of others. This supporting evidence shows that being bold leads to better business. In fact, the companies that made the right bold moves increased their odds of moving to the top quintile of corporate performers by up to 47 percent. From a corporate strategy perspective, the article explains five big moves that companies can take 1) Active resource reallocation, 2) Strong capital programs, 3) Distinctive productivity improvement, 4) Differentiation improvements, and 5) Programmatic merger and acquisition. These corporate chess moves may sound like Swahili for those not as familiar with the language of corporate finance. Still, they are difficult decisions and courageous choices that, according to the article, are required by CEOs and boards. Boldness. The article continues:

"I know that big moves feel scary. Over decades of interacting with business leaders, I've often seen teams start with high ambitions only to have risk aversion eat away at them. The CEO may focus on the quarter rather than the decade ahead. Managers worry that failing to achieve a big target will affect their careers. Even successful entrepreneurs can turn cautious, wary of putting what they built in peril . . . To fend off such tendencies, keep in mind that four of the five big moves are asymmetric; in other words, the upside opportunity far outweighs the downside risk. And the more big moves you make, the more you raise your chances of outperformance."

That reminds me of another example of Being Bold that hits closer to home for me. As I mentioned earlier, I currently live in Sydney, Australia. Personally, it felt like a bold move for me to relocate to Sydney from my humble existence in Texas, but that is not what I'm referring to. This is a story of boldness that my fellow Aussies would term "backing yourself." It is a story of personal ambition and a bold belief mixed in with a dose of faith . . . the kind of bold faith fairy tales are made of.

It all started with the current created from the gathering I mentioned in Tool #8: Be Agile with the meeting of minds that created the Agile manifesto. For those who need a reminder, Agile is the software development methodology now used by companies like NASA, Apple, and Google that hopes to improve the way software is delivered. This story continued from that Agile movement when a couple of college friends started a tech company in Sydney.

Scott Farquhar and Mike Cannon-Brookes had a belief in the future of Agile and knew that people and organizations would need technology to help support the movement. At the age of twenty-two, Farquhar and Cannon-Brookes made the bold move to start a software company in 2002 with $10,000 on a credit card. This was more than youthful excitement and naive ambition; it was boldness in action. The pair had more than a few obstacles and challenges in front of them. They had just witnessed the dot-com crash. Farquhar had just turned down a job with the prestigious accounting firm Price Waterhouse Cooper. They were starting the company in Sydney, Australia, which had no software industry, so this meant access to tech talent and funding was scarce. But convinced of the future success of Agile, their company was started with simple beliefs: "We're for teams!" and "Don't f#@! the customer!" Cannon-Brookes and Farquhar had an idea that their boldness was going to pay dividends when they racked up sales of over 1.3 million by 2003 with their first simple product designed to help project teams work more collaboratively. Fast-forward to 2019, and the company, Atlassian, built by Aussies that "backed themselves," was reportedly worth more than fifty billion dollars and had offices across the world, including Amsterdam, Austin, and Bangalore.

So what does this have to do with your journey as a leader? In short, everything. As a leader in your career, your family, or your community, you will need to make bold steps, bold moves, and bold decisions at some point. There is no escaping this truth. I'm not only referring to the dramatic things, like pulling someone from a burning vehicle or taking the risk to start a billion-dollar company with your credit card. To Be Bold in the context of 10LT is to make small but courageous moves as part of your daily life. To Be Bold is to conquer the feeling of shame and tell your story anyway, which will likely have a positive effect on your team. To Be Bold is to volunteer your time even when you don't have the time to give. To Be Bold is to whisper, "I love you," even when you are mad. To Be Bold in daily life means hearing your voice quiver while your eyes well up with tears, but through it all, you find the strength to speak the words anyway. We are bold, brave, and courageous in so many ways. But how do we use this as a tool? How can boldness help me be a better leader or improve my family or my team?

A bold leader is someone who has the capacity to lead themselves or others to be the best version of themselves. To be a bold leader is to help others *live* as an alternative to surviving. To Be Bold requires an attitude of belief mixed with elements of action. To Be Bold as a tool, you must look at your world as an opportunity to live.

I have a mantra that I've been using for over a decade to help myself Be Bold with the choices that I make and the steps that I take. It is another way for us to look at this concept of being a bold leader. The mantra is actually more of a mnemonic device for BOLD: "Believe in Opportunity-Led Decisions." This is another tool within Tool #10 that can help you take bold steps daily. To Believe in Opportunity-Led Decisions is to believe that whatever life throws at you or whatever situation you are faced with, you can see that challenge as an opportunity to use all of the tools you've mastered to help make decisions. Some of those will be big, brave, courageous decisions; others will be insignificant ones. But practicing BOLD in our daily lives gets us match-fit and ready for the major moments when bold actions could be life-changing. "But KG, I don't get it. What are the steps I need to take to Be Bold?" The truth is, there is no magic spell. There is no secret ingredient. It all starts with simple belief. But the journey to Be Bold can be a long and winding road, just like being a leader. However, to make it simple for the list-lovers out there, I have assembled five keys to help you make bold moves during your leader's journey.

1. Have clear purpose and priorities: We have learned about how to manage purpose and priorities with POT (Purpose Over Task) and POC (Priority, Order, and Consistency); therefore, our boldness should align with our goals when possible.

2. Pair your actions with context: Use your unique situation and personal journey as a superpower to inform your decisions and take action. You have been blessed with the life you have lived for a reason. Your knowledge and experiences (good and bad) have given you a unique opportunity to act.

3. Acknowledge the risks: When looking to go against the grain, you must understand the potential impacts, both positive and negative. Doing anything less is foolish and not bold. But remember that being overly risk-averse can work against you. Referring back to the article regarding business success, this line stands out: "The upside opportunity far outweighs the downside risk."

4. Mentally manage the fear of failure: Use BOLD techniques to dampen fears. I try hard to believe in opportunities over the fear of failure.
- Say, "I want a raise," over "I might get denied."
- Say, "I want to be a leader," over "What if people don't respect me?"
- Say, "I want to meet more people," over "What if I'm embarrassed if I don't have the right words to say?"

- Say, "I want to be my own boss," over "What if I don't make enough money?"
- Say, "I want to be a musician," over "What if they don't like my music?"
- Like Purpose Over Task (POT), be guided by the opportunity.

5. Don't hesitate: My brother once told me, "If you think long, you think wrong," so I've always taken this to heart. This means the longer you think about something, the more likely it is for that decision to be wrongly based on fear instead of opportunity. Make moves knowing that agility is now an active part of your toolkit; therefore, action and adjustment are better than no action or waiting for everything to be perfect.

How would you describe yourself? Are you bold? Do you make bold choices in your life, in your career, in your business? On a scale of 1 to 10, with 10 being the highest, where do you sit on the boldness scale? What dreams have you been talking yourself out of? What business move are you on the fence about? What course or training have you been putting off? What situation needs your voice? What situation needs you to step forward toward the unknown? Where you sit on the scale is less important than recognizing the need to Be Bolder in your life and, more importantly, shaping and sharpening that boldness as a lifelong tool. To Be Bold means permitting yourself to use the tools that you have and putting them into action. As John A. Shedd wrote, "A ship in harbor is safe, but that is not what ships are built for."

IN RETROSPECT

Tool #10—Be Bold

- This is a tool about considering the risks but taking action anyway.
- To Be Bold means making the big moves that are required to be successful.
- We learned to Believe in Opportunity-Led Decisions (BOLD).
- We heard that being Bold is less risky than doing nothing.
- To Be Bold requires taking action, one step at a time.

Practice Leading by Being Bold

1. What are the big moves that you have avoided in your personal life? Take a moment to refocus your energy on making choices that have been in the back of your mind. With your thoughts focused, decide what four big moves you can make in the next ten days.

2. Take the time to write down five potential moves that could kickstart or transform your career. Narrow the list to the three with the most significant impact. Then hold yourself to the commitment of making one bold career move this week. The crucial part is taking the first step.

> A GOOD TOOL IMPROVES THE WAY YOU WORK. A GREAT TOOL IMPROVES THE WAY YOU THINK.
>
> —JEFF DUNTEMANN

CONCLUSION

Think Differently

IT DEPENDS

Why are people so obsessed with home improvement shows? I ask myself this regularly as I flip through the pages and pages of cable, satellite, and streaming shows dedicated to the subject. Maybe it's the sense of fulfillment in seeing the dramatic transformations. Maybe it's the show's hosts and their colorful personalities. Or maybe it's because, within each home makeover episode, we see the things we would love to do in our own home or world if we had the tools, time, and—oh yeah—the experience.

Yes, we cannot forget that little thing that prevents the average home improvement wanna-be like me from ripping out that wall, moving that bathroom, or refurbishing the kitchen this weekend. We need the right tools, we need experience, and depending on the level of experience, we need time. Now that we have finished discovering the 10LT, you can think of yourself as having the right tools—tick. Now, the next stage in the process is to take the time to use, refine, and gain experience with each of the tools.

I was once asked the question: "Will these tools make me a better leader?" My response at the time was a rambling, noncommittal answer about "putting in the work to be a better leader." I'm not great with impromptu answers, but I'm working on it. Upon reflection, that answer, although "soft," as my older brother would say, is not entirely incorrect. Along with first acknowledging and recognizing yourself as a leader, it does take work to be a leader and even more work to be a good leader. But if I had that question to address again, I'd probably answer the question like a true consultant and respond with another question, or more accurately, a series of questions. I would have retorted with: "Does giving a surgeon better tools make her a better surgeon? Does giving a mechanic better tools make him a better mechanic? Does giving our teachers better tools to teach our next generation of leaders potentially make them better teachers?"

The answer is simple yet complex. In summary, I'd say, "It depends." Again, it's a typical consultant answer. Do I believe that giving a good surgeon better tools to work more efficiently, more precisely, or to have a more comprehensive view of her patient's condition can make her a better surgeon? Absolutely. But if a surgical resident or intern has all the same tools, yes, they have the opportunity to be made better. The resident has been given tools that can improve the way they work. But the resident still must put the time and effort in to become as skilled and accomplished as the other more experienced surgeons. In truth, it is not the tool alone that makes the experienced surgeon better. She becomes a better surgeon not by simply reading about how the tool works. She becomes a better practitioner by knowing both when to use each tool and how to use the tool to her advantage. She recognizes the tool and knows the best way to make that tool benefit both her and her patient. As I said, it depends. It depends on how much effort, how many hours, and how many steps the surgeon-in-training is willing to take to improve. The same applies to the mechanic and the teacher. The benefit of any tool is only realized by each of them understanding the best situation for using a tool.

Let's get back to the original question: "Will the tools of 10LT make me a better leader?" The right tools can and will make a big difference in the right hands. But they are not shortcuts or a fast-track to leadership. Trust me, I've tried many things hoping to shorten the process, but a shortcut doesn't exist. However, 10LT will give anyone looking to improve in life or as a leader a huge step forward, but it still takes work. For those new leaders or those unsure that this leadership stuff is for them, these tools are designed to give you the best possible start to your journey. The next step is yours.

ON THE WAY YOU THINK

"Mr. Watson, come here! I want to see you." These were the words uttered by Alexander Graham Bell on his new electronic device—the telephone. Bell said that phrase to his assistant, Thomas A. Watson, in the next room of their Boston laboratory in 1876. Watson then confirmed that he could hear Bell's now-famous words. And with that, the first telephone was brought into the world. Bell was awarded the first patent for the telephone, although he stumbled upon the invention while originally hoping to create an improvement to the telegraph, which had already been established for over thirty years. The telegraph could only send one signal at a time, so Bell planned to create the first working multisignal telegraph. Bell's idea was to create what he called a harmonic telegraph that used varied electronic currents to create variable audible frequencies. This was inspired by his many years of working with the nature of sound and auditory improvements since both his mother and wife were hearing impaired. Fortunately for us, he failed to create a better version of the telegraph, but I'd say we are all better off for it. Yes, the telephone was born fortuitously, thanks to Bell's ability to think creatively. He used all of his tools and experiences to create something magical. It was Bell's years of teaching deaf children to speak, along with his passion for discovering auditory improvements combined with the talents of a young electrical specialist, Watson, that made it all come together. Bell could see the possibilities through the lens of his many experiences that made the telephone possible.

Bell had a feeling that his discovery was a big deal. As the idea started to gain momentum, his grand vision was that the telephone could one day be used as a person-to-person communication tool, eventually replacing the telegraph. He even dreamed that one day the phone would ultimately be wired to every home, like electricity. What would Alexander Graham Bell think of his humble communication tool today? The telephone had changed from a wire between two adjoining rooms in a Boston laboratory, to connecting cities across America by

1915, then on to ultimately revolutionizing both computing and communication internationally with today's smartphones. It's grown from a tool with the sole purpose of connecting people through a static-filled audio signal to a modern tool of conveniences like unlocking our car doors or connecting to our smart homes. The telephone has evolved as a tool. Like any great tool, it has changed both the way we work and the way we think. The same should be true of the tools in this book. Each chapter in 10LT is not only meant to provide practical rules, tools, and habits for life and leading. Each tool is planted as a seed for your thoughts and has the potential to grow. Each tool has the potential to help us grow as leaders, grow as friends, grow as students, grow as parents, and grow as partners.

These tools have been selected for their ability to help you think differently about the world around you. Each tool, when applied in context with your situation and background, can help improve and evolve your thinking. Even if you are already familiar with tools like Purpose Over Task, Be Vanilla, or Be Agile, this book should serve as an ongoing reference that expands on your existing knowledge, expands on the possibilities, and expands your beliefs. Bell did not intend to create the social current that eventuated into the iPhone, touted by Jobs and the smartphones of today. He had a simple belief that he could make a difference, then took steps to fulfill that purpose.

As we draw to the close of this book, I hope you will use this example from Bell to imagine how far tools can take you. And not only the tools from this book. Imagine what other ideas you can use as a tool within your career, family, or community. Imagine what you can discover. Like our prehistoric ancestors who dared to imagine a rock could be an implement to hammer with, then on to our medieval forefathers, who believed the same rock could form castle walls. We have the uniquely human ability to expand our thinking. I hope these pages allow you to expand your bubble of belief and imagine what is possible in your world. As I mentioned before, 10LT was never intended to be simply a list of tools. This book is designed to help you take the next step forward in your journey as a leader. Whether you are a seasoned executive or a reluctant leader, the opportunity for growth is the same. No matter where you are starting from as a leader, 10LT is about providing the tools to help you think differently than you did before.

We learned to think differently about what it means to be a leader when we discussed my views on leading as part of your career, family, and community. We understand that the modern elements of a leader include connection, communication, curiosity, commitment, and context. We learned to think about managing **Purpose Over Task** (Tool #1). Also, when we **Learn a New Language** (Tool #2), we can **Tell Different Stories** (Tool #3). Our eyes were opened to how we can **Create Currents** (Tool #4) in our world while never forgetting to **Play** (Tool #5). We also learned the value of pause, meditation, and thoughtful reflection through the power of **Pulse** (Tool #6). We then learned how to **Be Vanilla** by adopting habits that could make a big difference (Tool #7). We adjusted our thinking to **Be Agile** (Tool #8) in a world of constant change. Then we learned how to think differently about ourselves, to **Be Real** leaders (Tool #9), and how to believe in ourselves and **Be Bold** leaders (Tool #10). Yes, we've learned a lot about ourselves and how to respond differently to the world around us.

If this information has been overwhelming and you don't even know where to start, then let me help by saying, "Start with the tool that is most helpful to you *right now*." If your goal is to connect more with your family or team, revisit tools like Learn a New Language (Tool #2), Tell Different Stories (Tool #3), or Be Real (Tool #9). If you need to think differently as an entrepreneur, consider concepts like Create Currents (Tool #4), Be Agile (Tool #8), and Be Bold (Tool #10). If you are no longer enjoying your personal or career situation, try to Use Purpose Over Task (Tool #1) or ways to Play (Tool #5). If you want to be more effective in your life goals, look at how you Pulse (Tool #6) or Be Vanilla (Tool #7).

Start with what can solve the most immediate need. Start small but start today. I once heard the story of a woman stranded in a desert. She had been separated from her travel convoy and wandered alone without water for three days. As the third day reached its hottest point, the woman spotted what appeared to be a lake in the distance. "Could it be true, or is it just a mirage?" she spoke to the vast desert. Although she was unsure if it was real, she used her last ounce of strength and staggered toward the lake. Her prayers were answered. This was no mirage. This was indeed a large lake filled with crystal-clear water. She was saved. There in front of her was more fresh water than she could drink in a lifetime. Yet the woman did not do what her body was pleading for. Although she was dying of thirst, she did not drink. Amazingly, she simply could not bring herself to drink the water. She stood at the water's edge and simply stared down at it.

A wise man was riding on a camel from a nearby desert town. He stopped after noticing the odd behavior of the lady kneeling at the foot of the lake. He got off the camel and drew closer to the woman. Being familiar with the brutality of the desert, he recognized the woman's desperate, tattered, and thirsty appearance. He slowly approached her and asked, "Are you okay? Why don't you have a drink?" She broke her gaze at the water and looked up with tears in her eyes. "I am dying of thirst," she said. "But there is way too much water here in this lake to drink. No matter what I do, I can't possibly finish it all."

The wise man smiled, kneeled beside her, and scooped some water with his cupped hands. He took a sip of the water for himself. Then he scooped another handful of water and offered it to the woman, saying, "Your opportunity now and for the rest of your life is to understand that you don't have to drink the whole lake to quench your thirst. You can take one sip and enjoy that sip for what it is. You can then decide to take another if you choose. Take a breath and drink. Focus only on the mouthful in front of you. Then your worry, anxiety, fear, and overwhelming feelings will gradually fade."

As you consider all that we have covered with 10LT, I suggest you take heed of the wise man's words. Take one sip at a time. Take one step toward the next part of your journey, then another. Take action on one small thing, then another. Don't be overwhelmed by what you have learned or read. Don't be anxious about the task ahead. Focus on the opportunity and your purpose—your purpose to lead.

Remember, I am on this learning and leading journey with you, so let's continue to explore together. To learn more about my leadership exploits and musings, connect with me directly at KGButlerMedia.com or join the leadership conversation through my blog and newsletter at LeadersToolbelt.com. For those who prefer audio, you can find the audiobook on Audible or listen to the Leaders Toolbelt or Leadership Decanted podcasts on your favorite app. You can also find me on social media channels, such as YouTube, LinkedIn, Twitter, Instagram, and Facebook.

What started as a personal journey of discovery, I pray, can Create Currents of change in you or in those around you. Along with my journey, we have looked at dozens of examples and stories of the tools in action. We have talked about record-setting aviators, spelling-bee champions, gymnastics superstars, researchers, presidents, space missions, psychologists, billion-dollar start-ups, and the happiest place on Earth. We have talked through many examples, but now you must choose to step forward in your journey. Now, imagine yourself having these stories, the tools of 10LT, and your own story as part of your personal toolbelt. The tools are always with you. You are armed and ready for the next intersection in your journey. Whatever direction you decide to take, I'm sure you will find purpose in your path. As philosopher Ralph Waldo Emerson so eloquently said, "The only person you are destined to become is the person you decide to be." The future is surely bright because you have decided to lead.

NOTES

In the following section, I have included the notes, citations, and references from each chapter of the book (the page number is listed). Leaders who are curious about the research or have a thirst for more will find this section useful. However, much of my research and information has been gathered over many years and quite often from various sources. This means some of the source material is in hardcopy, the information has been archived, or the original hyperlink locations are no longer available. In those cases, I have attempted to provide the most relevant reference that is searchable online for a more practical method of satisfying the curious.

Also, in an effort to make this section brief and more relevant, I have skipped notes for common text and quotes, dictionary definitions, and books where the title and author are well known.

Furthermore, I fully expect that I have made a mistake. If I have given credit to the wrong person or missed giving credit to someone for an idea, please contact me at info@kgbutlermedia.com. I'll attempt to clarify the issue or resolve it as quickly as possible.

Introduction: The Importance of Tools

8. Give them tools, they'll do wonderful things with them: Jeff Goodell, "Steve Jobs in 1994: The Rolling Stone Interview," Rolling Stone, January 17, 2011, https://www.rollingstone.com/culture/culture-news/steve-jobs-in-1994-the-rolling-stone-interview-231132/

10. Now try to imagine 2.6 million years ago, which is about the time when early stone toolmaking began: "What does it mean to be human? Stone Tools," Smithsonian National Museum of Natural History, February 3, 2022, https://humanorigins.si.edu/evidence/behavior/stone-tools

The Journey

18. We also couldn't fathom how no other vehicles were involved in the accident while the truck pinballed across I-20: Chandler Brown, "Two pull man from Truck," The Atlanta Journey-Constitution, August 19, 2000

Modern Leaders

28. The Great Man Theory: Thomas Carlyle, "The Great Man Theory of Leadership Explained," Villanova University, September 10, 2021, https://www.villanovau.com/resources/leadership/great-man-theory/

> "Universal History, the history of what man has accomplished in this world, is at bottom the History of the Great Men who have worked here. They were the leaders of men, these great ones; the modellers, patterns, and in a wide sense creators, of whatsoever the general mass of men contrived to do or to attain; all things that we see standing accomplished in the world are properly the outer material result, the practical realization and embodiment, of Thoughts that dwelt in the Great Men sent into the world: the soul of the whole world's history, it may justly be considered, were the history of these." May 05, 1840, https://www.gutenberg.org/files/1091/1091-h/1091-h.htm#link2H_4_0002

28. Autocratic, democratic, and laissez-faire: psychologist Kurt Lewin, "Patterns of aggressive behavior in experimentally created social climates," Journal of Social Psychology, May 1939, https://tu-dresden.de/mn/psychologie/ipep/lehrlern/ressourcen/dateien/lehre/lehramt/lehrveranstaltungen/Lehrer_Schueler_Interaktion_SS_2011/Lewin_1939_original.pdf?lang=en

32. **This concept of adapting your leadership style was first popularized by Paul Hersey and Ken Blanchard as they introduced the Situational Leadership Theory in the 1960s:** Paul Hersey & Ken Blanchard, "Management of Organizational Behaviour: Utilizing Human Resources," Prentice-Hall, May 1969, https://www.amazon.com/Management-Organizational-Behavior-Utilizing-1969-05-03/dp/B01F9G2E7Q#detailBullets_feature_div

Tool #1: Use Purpose Over Task

45. **Walt Disney and his brother, Roy, started Disney Brothers Studio in the early 1920s:** Editors of Encyclopaedia, "Disney Company," Encyclopedia Britannica, December 13, 2021, https://www.britannica.com/topic/Disney-Company

50. **So, in this instance, Jenny chose purpose versus task:** Disney Institute, "A value, knows as 'task versus... - Disney Institute | Facebook," Facebook, August 25, 2011, https://m.facebook.com/DisneyInstitute/posts/239723542739486?locale2=en_US&_rdr

52. **Baader-Meinhof phenomenon, the psychological theory behind buying a red car then suddenly noticing red cars everywhere:** Kate Kershner, "What's the Baader-Meinhof Phenomenon?" HowStuffWorks.com, March 20, 2015, https://science.howstuffworks.com/life/inside-the-mind/human-brain/baader-meinhof-phenomenon.htm

55. **I'm helping put a man on the moon, Mr. President:** Knowledge@Wharton (upenn.edu), "Meaningful Work: What Leaders Can Learn from NASA and the Space Race," Wharton School of the University of Pennsylvania, March 16, 2017, https://knowledge.wharton.upenn.edu/article/what-leaders-can-learn-from-nasa/

54. **I believe we should go to the moon. But I think every citizen of this country, as well as the members of the Congress, should consider the matter:** President John F Kennedy, "Special Message to the Congress on Urgent National Needs," NASA, May 25, 1961, https://www.nasa.gov/

vision/space/features/jfk_speech_text.html

55. **We choose to go to the moon in this decade and do the other things, not because they are easy, but because they are hard because that goal will serve to organize and measure the best of our energies and skills:** President John F Kennedy, "Address at Rice University on the Nation's Space Effort," September 12, 1962, https://spacecenter.org/exhibits-and-experiences/starship-gallery/kennedy-podium/

Tool #2: Learn a New Language

65. **This notion of a person's spoken language having a direct and profound impact**: Willett Kempton & Paul Kay, "What Is The Sapir-Whorf Hypothesis," American Anthropological Association, 1984, https://anthrosource.onlinelibrary.wiley.com/doi/pdf/10.1525/aa.1984.86.1.02a00050

66. **According to explorer Franz Boas, Inuktitut, the Inuit Eskimo language, has many more words that all describe "snow.":** Franz Boas, "Introduction to Handbook of American Indian Languages Part 1," Government Printing Office, 1911, https://library.si.edu/digital-library/book/bulletin4011911smit

66. **The Eskimos' perception of snow is colored by a myriad of nuances related to how the snow is falling, the effects of the wind, and every other detailed variation relative to the Inuit language:** Benjamin Whorf, "Science and Linguistics," The Technology Review, April 1940, https://www.mit.edu/~allanmc/whorf.scienceandlinguistics.pdf

73. **A study by a group at the Wharton School of the University of Pennsylvania demonstrated this impact:** Adam M Grant and Francesca Gino, "A little thanks goes a long way: Explaining why gratitude expressions motivate prosocial behavior," Journal of Personal and Social Psychology, June 6, 2010, https://doi.apa.org/PsycARTICLES/journal/psp/98/6

75. **Have a read of this excerpt from the great orator Winston Churchill as an example:** Winston Churchill, "We Shall Fight On The Beaches," Speech given on June 4, 1940, https://winstonchurchill.org/resources/speeches/1940-the-finest-hour/we-shall-fight-on-the-beaches/

76. A recent study led by Psychologist Megan Robbins of the University of California Riverside helps confirm this thinking: A. Karan, R. Rosenthal, & M. L. Robbins, "Meta-analytic evidence that we-talk predicts relationship and personal functioning in romantic couples," Journal of Social and Personal Relationships, September 9, 2019, https://doi.org/10.1177/0265407518795336 page 2624-2651

Tool #3: Tell Different Stories

82. Post was born in 1898: Erik D. Carlson, "Post, Wiley Hardeman," The Encyclopedia of Oklahoma History and Culture, date unknown, https://www.okhistory.org/publications/enc/entry?entry=PO023

84. This current of wind would later be known as the jet stream: Stephen Sherman, "Wiley Post: First to Fly Solo Around the World, Lost over Alaska," Acepilots.com, January 2011, http://acepilots.com/post.html

85. Our brains are chemically changed when exposed to a good story: Dr. Paul J Zak, "How Stories Change The Brain," Greater Good Magazine, Berkeley University of California, December 2013, https://greatergood.berkeley.edu/article/item/how_stories_change_brain

86. Stories that capture our attention can also produce a chemical called cortisol. In our brains, cortisol is often associated with distress: Arefa Cassoobhoy, MD, "What is Cortisol?" WebMD, December 13, 2020, https://www.webmd.com/a-to-z-guides/what-is-cortisol

86. It also turns out that a good story can lead to commitment or taking action: Dr. Paul J Zak, "Empathy, Neurochemistry and the Dramatic Arc," YouTube, October 2012, https://youtu.be/dSyyAcrsnT4

93. If we look at the Bible in its entirety, some accounts show over two thousand other characters being mentioned through its tales and parables: https://www.bible.com/en-GB

Tool #4: Create Currents

99. Balu Natarajan correctly spelled the final word needed to be crowned the champion: "m-i-l-i-e-u wins," Nashua Telegraph, June 7, 1985, https://news.google.com/newspapers?nid=2209&dat=19850607&id=2ZorAAAAIBAJ&sjid=ovoFAAAAIBAJ&pg=5449,1208962&hl=en

105. Bubble of belief: Tytus Michalski, "5 Questions With Dave Gray: Liminal Thinking, Doom Loops, Attention, Beliefs, Filter Bubbles & More," Fusion by Fresco Capital, Feb 2, 2017, https://medium.com/fusion-by-fresco-capital/5-questions-with-dave-gray-liminal-thinking-doom-loops-attention-beliefs-filter-bubbles-more-2cd82366a520

101. Durkheim coined the term social currents when describing the impact of the conscious collective: Emile Durkheim, "The Rules of Sociological Method," The Free Press, 1982, https://monoskop.org/images/1/1e/Durkheim_Emile_The_Rules_of_Sociological_Method_1982.pdf

103. Bannister became the first person in history to accomplish the mythical "4-minute mile: unknown author, "Roger Bannister: First sub-four-minute mile," Guinness Book of World Records, date unknown, https://www.guinnessworldrecords.com/records/hall-of-fame/first-sub-four-minute-mile

106. In the 2014 article, Fritz and his team of Austrian conservationists studied the origins of the iconic V-shape: Ed Yong, "Birds That Fly in a V Formation Use An Amazing Trick," National Geographic, January 16, 2017, https://www.nationalgeographic.com/science/article/birds-that-fly-in-a-v-formation-use-an-amazing-trick

108. Studies show that the leading bird in a classic V-shape is often working up to 20 percent harder than the other birds: Portugal, S., Hubel, T., Fritz, J. et al. "Upwash exploitation and downwash avoidance by flap phasing in ibis formation flight." Nature 505, 2014. https://doi.org/10.1038/nature12939

Tool #5: Play (PLAy)

122. Brown describes play in his book: Stuart Brown, "Play: How it Shapes the Brain, Opens the Imagination, and Invigorates the Soul,"

Scribe Publications, June 28, 2010, https://www.amazon.com.au/Play-Shapes-Brain-Imagination-Invigorates/dp/1921640537/ref=sr_1_1?crid=2VCEKP7LSKZ7K&keywords=stuart+brown+play&qid=1647317005&sprefix=stuart+brown+play%2Caps%2C201&sr=8-1

123. **Play can release the chemicals in our brain that create lasting empathic connections:** Crystal Raypole, "How to Hack Your Hormones for a Better Mood," HealthLine Media, September 30, 2019, https://www.healthline.com/health/happy-hormone

Tool #6: Pulse

133. **Your heart beats over 100,000 times per day:** Nova, "Amazing Heart Facts," PBS, date unknown, https://www.pbs.org/wgbh/nova/heart/heartfacts.html#:~:text=Your%20heart%20beats%20about%20100%2C000,blood%20out%20to%20the%20body

134. **The first person credited with measuring or timing the pulse was Herophilus of Alexandria, Egypt:** Editors of Encyclopaedia. "Herophilus," Encyclopedia Britannica, November 30, 2018, https://www.britannica.com/biography/Herophilus

137. **Studies show that including routine meditation can reduce mental stress and anxiety:** Mayo Clinic Staff, "Meditation: A simple, fast way to reduce stress," Mayo Clinic, April 22, 2020, https://www.mayoclinic.org/tests-procedures/meditation/in-depth/meditation/art-20045858#:~:text=Meditation%20can%20produce%20a%20deep,physical%20and%20emotional%20well%2Dbeing

138. **Adult cheetahs can be over 1.5 yards in length and weigh well over one hundred pounds:** Smithsonian Staff, "Cheetah," Smithsonian's National Zoo & Conservation Biology Institute, date unknown, https://nationalzoo.si.edu/animals/cheetah

Tool #7: Be Vanilla

150. Once a flowering orchid is located, the flower must be pollinated

by hand through a delicate technique discovered in 1841 and still used today: Rebecca Rupp, "The History of Vanilla," National Geographic, October 23, 2014, https://www.nationalgeographic.com/culture/article/plain-vanilla

150. It was the eyewatering price tag and the meteoric rise of the lowly vanilla pod to over $600: C.D., "Why there is a worldwide shortage of vanilla," The Economist, March 28, 2018, https://www.economist.com/the-economist-explains/2018/03/28/why-there-is-a-worldwide-shortage-of-vanilla

151. Vanilla beans to make an ice cream recipe, which still resides with other historical artifacts in the Library of Congress: "Thomas Jefferson, no date, Ice Cream Recipe," Library of Congress, date unknown (circa 1800), https://www.loc.gov/resource/mtj1.056_0146_0146/

152. In comparison, vanilla ice cream with its colorless, smooth texture was ordinary: Amanda Fortini, "Vanilla is anything but plain," Herald-Tribune, January 21, 2014, https://www.heraldtribune.com/story/news/2014/01/22/vanilla-is-anything-but-plain/29224433007/

154. 2014 commencement speech given at the University of Texas in Austin by former Navy SEAL Admiral William H. McRaven: University Communications, "Adm. McRaven Urges Graduates to Find Courage to Change the World," UT News, May 16, 2014, https://news.utexas.edu/2014/05/16/mcraven-urges-graduates-to-find-courage-to-change-the-world/

156. James Clear, author of Atomic Habits, recommends habit stacking: James Clear, "Atomic Habits: An Easy & Proven Way to Build Good Habits & Break Bad Ones," Avery, October 16, 2018, https://jamesclear.com/atomic-habits

156. Inspired by a concept known as "big rocks," popularized by Stephen Covey: Stephen Covey, "Big Rocks - Stephen R. Covey," Franklin Covey Co., 1994, https://resources.franklincovey.com/the-8th-habit/big-rocks-stephen-r-covey

Tool #8: Be Agile

166. **The Biles," as it's called in gymnastic circles, was created by turning a point of potential weakness, the injury, into a strength:** Jeff Haden, "Simone Biles and the 'Biles': How to Turn a Weakness Into Innovation and Excellence," Inc., date unknown, https://www.inc.com/jeff-haden/simone-biles-and-the-biles-how-to-turn-a-weakness-into-innovation-and-excellence.html

167. **In 2001, a group of software developers from across the US gathered in Snowbird, Utah:** Kent Beck, Mike Beedle, Arie van Bennekum, Alistair Cockburn, Ward Cunningham, Martin Fowler, James Grenning, Jim Highsmith, Andrew Hunt, Ron Jeffries, Jon Kern, Brian Marick, Robert C. Martin, Steve Mellor, Ken Schwaber, Jeff Sutherland & Dave Thomas "Manifesto for Agile Software Development," February 11-13, 2001, https://agilemanifesto.org/history.html

170. **In the research paper by Dr. Darren Good and Dr. Bauback Yeganeh**: Darren Good & Bauback Yeganeh, "Cognitive Agility: Adapting to Real-time Decision Making at Work," OD Practioner Review Vol 44, No 2, 2012, https://cdn.ymaws.com/www.odnetwork.org/resource/resmgr/odp/odp-v44,no2-good_yeganeh.pdf

175. **A study of wild cheetah pursuits showed that of 192 hunts:** James Fair, "Apex predators in the wild: which mammals are the most dangerous," BBC Wildlife, November 24, 2021, https://www.discoverwildlife.com/animal-facts/mammals/hunting-success-rates-how-predators-compare/

177. **One of my favorite techniques for using agility is the decision cycle developed by Colonel John Boyd of the US Air Force:** Robert Coram, "Boyd: The Fighter Pilot Who Changed the Art of War," Little Brown & Co., April 15, 2004, https://www.amazon.com.au/Boyd-Fighter-Pilot-Who-Changed/dp/0316796883

Tool #9: Be Real

185. **Nowhere is this concept of valuing imperfections better illustrated than with the ancient Japanese art form called Kintsugi.:** Casey Lesser, "The Centuries-Old Japanese Tradition of Mending Broken Ceramics with Gold," Artsy.net, August 24, 2018, https://www.artsy.net/article/

artsy-editorial-centuries-old-japanese-tradition-mending-broken-ceramics-gold

186. In the world of computer technology, there is a coding practice called WYSIWYG: John Markoff, "The Real History of WYSIWYG," NY Times, October 18, 2007, https://bits.blogs.nytimes.com/2007/10/18/the-real-history-of-wysiwyg/

188. Brené Brown, loosely describes vulnerability as uncertainty and emotional exposure in her books Daring Greatly and Dare to Lead: Brené Brown, "Dare to Lead: Brave Work. Tough Conversations. Whole Hearts." Random House, October 9, 2018, https://www.amazon.com.au/Dare-Lead-Brave-Conversations-Hearts/dp/0399592520

191. In one study, Kurt Dirks and Donald Ferrin collected research on trust in leadership from over four decades of data: Donald L. Ferrin & Kurt Dirks, "Trust in Leadership: Meta-Analytic Findings and Implications for Research and Practice," Journal of Applied Psychology, September 2002, https://www.researchgate.net/publication/11202113_Trust_in_Leadership_Meta-Analytic_Findings_and_Implications_for_Research_and_Practice

191. There is evidence of this in other research by Jack Zenger and Joseph Folkman, authors of Speed: John Zenger & Joseph Folkman, "Speed: How Leaders Accelerate Successful Execution," McGraw Hill, December 1, 2016, https://www.amazon.com/Speed-Leaders-Accelerate-Successful-Execution/dp/1259837386

Tool #10: Be Bold

203. Bold Moves Are Less Risky Than a Timid Corporate Strategy" explains the benefits of businesses making bold moves: Sven Smit, "Bold moves are less risky than a timid corporate strategy," McKinsey & Company, March 6, 2018, https://www.mckinsey.com/business-functions/strategy-and-corporate-finance/our-insights/the-strategy-and-corporate-finance-blog/bold-moves-are-less-risky-than-a-timid-corporate-strategy

204. Farquhar and Cannon-Brookes made the bold move to start a software company in 2002 with $10,000 on a credit card.: Denham

Sadler, "Atlassian Story: Atlassian story: How two indebted suburban guys from Sydney created a $US 3 billion tech juggernaut," September 28, 2015, https://www.smartcompany.com.au/startupsmart/advice/startupsmart-growth/atlassian-story-how-two-indebted-suburban-guys-from-sydney-created-a-us-3-billion-tech-juggernaut/

Conclusion: Think Differently

213. Mr. Watson, come here! I want to see you.: David Hochfelder, "Alexander Graham Bell," Encyclopedia Britannica, February 27, 2022, https://www.britannica.com/biography/Alexander-Graham-Bell

INDEX

A

Agile Software 167
Aldrin, Buzz 55
Am I too full 146
Angelou, Maya 196
Apple 7, 8, 204
Armstrong, Neil 55
Atlassian 205

B

Baader-Meinhof phenomenon 52
Baker and a Farmer 189, 190
Banister, Roger 103, 111
Basso, Dan 71
Be Agile 5, 165, 166, 169, 172, 173, 176, 177, 178, 179, 191, 202, 204, 215, 216, 217
  Practice 179
Bearded Bakers 125
Be Bold 197, 201, 202, 203, 204, 205, 206, 208, 209, 216, 217
  Five keys 207, 208
  Practice 209
Bell, Alexander Graham 213, 214, 215
Bennis, Warren G. 27
Be Real 183, 186, 187, 188, 189, 190, 192, 194, 202, 216, 217, 229
  Practice 194
Be Vanilla 149, 152, 153, 155, 156, 158, 159, 161, 162, 172, 191, 192, 215, 216, 217, 228
  Practice 162
Biles, Simone 165, 166, 172, 173, 179, 229
Blanchard, Ken 32, 33, 223
Boas, Franz 66, 224
Boyd, John 177, 178
Brown, Stuart 122, 123
Bryant, Kobe 165
Burberry 203
Burrell Tibbs Flying Circus 83

C

Canadian National Railway 203
Cannon-Brookes, Mike 204, 205
Churchill, Winston 75, 76, 77, 116
Claremont Graduate University Center for Neuroeconomics Studies 85
Clear, James 156
Cognitive agility 169, 170, 171
Cognitive challenges 95

Cohen, Alan 132
Corning Inc 203
Covey, Stephen 156, 158, 182
Create Currents 99, 100, 101, 103, 104, 107, 110, 111, 113, 114, 118, 202, 216, 217, 219
  local currents 102, 110
  Practice 114
Currents Matter 109, 110

D

Davis, Gerard 104
Defense Advantage Research Projects Agency (DARPA) 86
Dirks, Kurt 191
Disney Institute 45
Disney, Walt and Roy 45
Dorsett, Tony 165
Duntemann, Jeff 210
Durant, Will 148
Durkheim, Emile 101, 102

E

Earhart, Amelia 84
El-issa, Ameer, Joey and Mouna 126
Emerson, Ralph Waldo 78, 219
E. W. Scripps Company 100
  National Spelling Bee 99, 100

F

Farquhar, Scott 204, 205
Fear of Failure 173, 174, 179, 207

Ferrin, Donald 191
Finding the Words 65
Folkman, Joseph 191, 192
Fritz, Johannes 106

G

Gagarin, Yuri 54
Gatty, Harold 83
GIO 72, 73, 75, 77, 79
  Gratitude 72, 73, 74, 79
  Interdependence 72, 75
  Optimism 16, 72, 75, 77
Goldsmith, Marshall 144
Good, Darren 170
Goodell, Jeff 7
Google 204
Great Man Theory 28

H

Harvard Business Review 191
Hemingway, Ernest 185
Herophilus of Alexandria 134
Hersey, Paul 32, 33

I

Illuminate your authentic story 88
Indianapolis Motor Speedway, 107
Inuktitut 66

J

James, William 54
Jesus of Nazareth 93

Jobs, Steve 8, 9
Jones, James Earl 128

K

Kennedy, John F. 11, 42, 54, 55
King, Martin Luther, Jr. 14, 71
Kintsugi 185, 194
Knafeh Bakery 126, 127

L

Landy, John 103, 111
LA Riots
 1992 101
 2020 101
Leadership Styles
 Autocratic 28, 29, 32, 35
 Democratic 28, 29, 32, 35
 Laissez-faire 28, 29, 32
 Leader's Triangle 33, 36, 37, 39, 108
 Career 37
 Community 38, 39
 Family 37, 38
 Learn a New Language 61, 79, 118, 216, 217
 Practice 79
Lewin, Kurt 28, 29
Lindbergh, Charles 84
Line of Sight Currents 106, 111
LinkedIn 105, 219
Low battery moments 141

M

Margolis, Michael 80
Marvel Universe 89

McAlindon, Harold 98
McKinsey & Company 203
McRaven, William H. 154
Messi, Lionel 165
Michelet, Jules 60
Modern Leaders Model 34, 35, 36, 40
Montgomery bus boycott 9
Multipurpose tools 70

N

NASA 55, 204
NASCAR 107
Natarajan, Balu 99, 100, 102, 103, 110
National Institute of Play 122
Nemmani, Karthik 100
Neurodivergence 95
NeXT Inc. 7

O

Obama, Barack 71
OODA Loop 177, 178, 179
Opex 63, 64
Origin stories 89
Oxytocin 86, 123, 131

P

Parks, Rosa 9
Phillimon, But 105
Play 57, 117, 118, 119, 120, 122, 123, 124, 126, 128, 130, 131, 216, 217
 Practice 131
POC Principle 156, 158, 162, 207

Post, Wiley 82, 83, 84, 85, 86, 89, 91, 101, 130
Pulse 133, 134, 135, 136, 137, 138, 139, 140, 141, 142, 143, 144, 146, 147, 149, 175, 216, 217
 Concept of rest 143
 make Pulse a pattern 139
 Practice 147
Purpose-Led Attitude 126, 127, 131
Purpose Over Task (POT) 5, 43, 46, 51, 52, 53, 54, 55, 56, 57, 58, 118, 128, 168, 207, 208, 215, 216, 217
Put your pride aside 108

R

Ramachandran, Rageshree 100
Renaldo, Cristiano 165
Respond to change over following a plan 168
Reynolds, Burt 183
Robbins, Megan 76
Rogers, Will 84
Rolling Stone magazine 7

S

Sanders, Barry 165
Sapir, Edward 65
Sapir-Whorf hypothesis 65
Shared language connection 69
Shaw, George Bernard 164
Situational Leadership Model 32
Sunk costs 63
Systemware Inc. 71

T

Tell Different Stories 81, 86, 87, 93, 95, 97, 118, 186, 191, 216, 217
 Practice 97
Tools
 Defining 117
 Refining 117, 118
Trust matters 190
Two-Way Trust 189

U

University of California Riverside 76
University of Pennsylvania Wharton School 73
University of Texas in Austin 154

V

V-formation 106, 108
Vision and Revision 176
Visualize the concept 129

W

Walt Disney Company 44, 45, 46, 47, 48, 49, 50, 223
Watson, Thomas A. 213
We talk 75, 76
Whorf, Benjamin Lee 65

Y

Yeganeh, Bauback 170

Yoshimasa, Ashikaga 185

Z

Zak, Paul J. 85, 86, 87
Zenger, Jack 191, 192
Zongo, Phillimon 105

INDEX

www.ingramcontent.com/pod-product-compliance
Lightning Source LLC
Chambersburg PA
CBHW050308010526
44107CB00055B/2156